Teacher's Guide to Tackling Attendance Challenges is an invaluable resource for developing an effective and sustainable strategy for reducing chronic absence. Combining research summaries and inspiring success stories with concrete advice, examples, and tools, it is a clear and compelling read that will help any administrator determine how to ensure students show up to class every day—so that they can learn and succeed.

Hedy N. Chang
Executive Director, Attendance Works

TEACHER'S *GUIDE TO*

TACKLING ATTENDANCE CHALLENGES

TEACHER'S *GUIDE TO*
TACKLING ATTENDANCE CHALLENGES

JESSICA **SPRICK** | TRICIA **BERG**

ASCD
Alexandria, Virginia USA

ancora PUBLISHING
Eugene, Oregon USA

ASCD®
1703 N. Beauregard St.
Alexandria, VA 22311-1714 USA
Phone: 800-933-2723 or 703-578-9600
Fax: 703-575-5400
Website: www.ascd.org • E-mail: member@ascd.org
Author guidelines: www.ascd.org/write

ancora PUBLISHING
21 West 6th Avenue
Eugene, OR 97401 USA
Phone: 866-542-1490
Fax: 541-345-1507
Website: www.ancorapublishing.com

Deborah S. Delisle, *Executive Director;* Stefani Roth, *Publisher;* Genny Ostertag, *Director, Content Acquisitions;* Susan Hills, *Acquisitions Editor*; Julie Houtz, *Director, Book Editing & Production;* Joy Scott Ressler, *Editor;* Judi Connelly, *Associate Art Director*; Masie Chong, *Graphic Designer;* Keith Demmons, *Production Designer*; Mike Kalyan, *Director, Production Services;* Trinay Blake, *E-Publishing Specialist*; Kelly Marshall, *Production Specialist.*

PAPERBACK ISBN: 978-1-4166-2714-2 ASCD product #118038 n2/19
PDF E-BOOK ISBN: 978-1-4166-2715-9

Quantity discounts are available: e-mail programteam@ascd.org or call 800-933-2723, ext. 5773, or 703-575-5773. For desk copies, go to www.ascd.org/deskcopy.

Library of Congress Cataloging-in-Publication Data

Names: Sprick, Jessica, author. | Berg, Tricia, author.
Title: Teacher's guide to tackling attendance challenges / Jessica Sprick and Tricia Berg.
Description: Alexandria, VA : ASCD, [2019] | Includes bibliographical references and index.
Identifiers: LCCN 2018039503 (print) | LCCN 2018055839 (ebook) | ISBN 9781416627159 (PDF) | ISBN 9781416627142 (pbk.) | ISBN 9781416627159 (ebk.)
Subjects: LCSH: School attendance--United States. | Classroom environment. | Teacher-student relationships. | Parent-teacher relationships. | Education--Parent participation--United States.
Classification: LCC LC143 (ebook) | LCC LC143 .S57 2019 (print) | DDC 371.2/94--dc23
LC record available at https://lccn.loc.gov/2018039503

27 26 25 24 23 22 21 20 19 1 2 3 4 5 6 7 8 9 10 11 12

TEACHER'S *GUIDE TO*
TACKLING ATTENDANCE CHALLENGES

Acknowledgments ix

Introduction 1

Chapter 1
Attendance—Not Another Competing Initiative 9

Chapter 2
Gathering and Analyzing the Right Data 19

Chapter 3
Speaking the Language of Attendance 40

Chapter 4
If You Want It, Teach It! Delivering Attendance Lessons 64

Chapter 5
Partnering with Families 87

Chapter 6
Implementing Effective Intervention Plans 101

Conclusion 117

Appendix A
Student Reinforcers 119

Appendix B
Handouts for Families 121

Bibliography 134

Index 138

About the Authors 144

Acknowledgments

Our thanks and appreciation to both ASCD and Ancora Publishing for agreeing to copublish this resource. Specifically, Susan Hills, Joy Scott Ressler, and the entire ASCD team, as well as Jody Kenyon Amato, Athena Lakri, and Elina Carmona, have provided support, guidance, and a true model of professional collegiality. From Ancora Publishing, Matt Sprick, Sara Ferris, and Natalie Conaway have provided invaluable assistance in guiding the development of this resource. Lastly, we owe deep debt to the many educators who field-tested our ideas and shared practical and creative ideas to enrich this book. Jake Alabiso, school psychologist from Barnes Elementary School, teachers Heather Graves and Jessica Morris, and John Calvert, school resource officer, provided inspiring models of what can happen when skilled leaders and dedicated staff work together to improve student attendance.

Introduction

For students to be successful in school, they have to actually be *in* school. As a classroom teacher, the work you do every day is vital to our nation's youth. But our students cannot learn and grow when they are not in school. Effective teachers develop a scope and sequence of instruction that builds across time. When students miss school, they miss vital building blocks of information. Effective teachers actively work to develop a classroom culture and climate that supports learning. When students are absent, they miss critical behavioral and social-emotional skills, as well as opportunities to build and maintain positive relationships with peers and adults. With each absence, whether excused or unexcused, students fall further and further behind. The good news is that you can improve these outcomes for students, and you play a powerful role in keeping our students in school.

You may be reading this book because your school or district is taking on an initiative to build a culture of attendance and eliminate chronic absence in your student body. Or perhaps you personally recognize that students in your class struggle with absenteeism. Whatever the reason, congratulations, both for recognizing that student success truly is dependent on being in school and for taking this important step in helping your students with this critical issue! You are part of a rapidly growing movement across the nation to address the pervasive issue of chronic absenteeism (defined as missing 10 percent of school days for any reason—excused absence, unexcused absence, or suspension). This resource provides concrete and practical strategies for teachers to implement in their own classrooms to address chronic absence and improve the attendance of all students.

Note from the Authors

We were both classroom teachers. We remember the difficulty of trying to maintain instructional momentum when students were constantly absent, the prep time lost in creating makeup work packets, and the struggle to catch students up when they fell behind due to absences. However, attendance was a bit of an "out of sight, out of mind" issue—often a lesser concern than issues like problematic behavior and failing to make adequate academic growth. We also remember feeling disempowered to really do anything about absences, especially those excused by parents.

We wish we had known what we know now—that absenteeism is equally as important to address as problematic behavior and academic difficulties, and that it *is* possible to effect meaningful change, even with excused absences! We have designed this book specifically for classroom teachers, with the recognition that your prep time and instructional time are stretched thin and precious to preserve. We hope you find that the practical strategies in this book are easy to implement and minimally invasive in terms of prep and class time, and that they make a significant difference in improving the attendance of all your students. Thank you for your time and energy in working to improve student attendance and giving your students the best opportunities for success in school and beyond!

—Jessica Sprick and Tricia Berg

The focus of this book is on creating a classroom culture of attendance. The first chapters will help you reduce the magnitude of attendance problems through universal prevention. You are likely to find that these strategies improve the attendance of all your students, from those with few absences to those who have frequent absences throughout the year. The later chapters focus on classroom interventions and ways to work with interventionists or multidisciplinary team supports to design and implement intervention plans. The goal is to reduce the number of students with problematic attendance in order to preserve intensive intervention resources (e.g., counselor/social worker support, multidisciplinary teams, wrap-around resources) for students with truly resistant and complex absenteeism problems.

This book advocates moving away from traditional approaches that have been used to address the problem of absenteeism. These approaches often do too little too late and focus on trying to punish away absenteeism problems.

The Traditional Approach

Although student absenteeism has long been recognized as a problem for many students, this issue has been largely overlooked in school and district efforts to improve student outcomes.

The Metric of Truancy

In a traditional approach to addressing absenteeism, schools look at measures of truancy to identify at-risk students. However, truancy relates only to absences that occur *without* parent permission. As you probably have observed, unexcused absences do not account for all or even the majority of absences for many students. Metrics of truancy can be misleading because many students have inordinate numbers of excused absences, especially in elementary school. Other students may have a relatively low rate of absenteeism for each type of reason (excused, unexcused, and suspension), but when the absences for different reasons are combined, these students exhibit patterns of problematic attendance. The extent of your students' absenteeism problems may not be apparent when you look solely at truancy metrics.

Increasingly Punitive "Interventions"

In a traditional model, when a student is identified as having an absenteeism problem, the following may occur:

- At a certain number of unexcused absences (e.g., three), a letter is sent home to warn the student and parent that unexcused absences can lead to truancy court proceedings.
- At a certain number of additional unexcused absences (e.g., five total), the school initiates a parent meeting by phone or conducts an in-person conference to further warn about the punitive consequences of additional unexcused absences.

- At a state-mandated level (e.g., 10 unexcused absences, or five in a one-month period), the school refers the student and student's family to juvenile court, and proceedings for a truancy hearing are initiated.
- If the court finds the student truant, the court orders penalties, such as:
  - Fines or other penalties for the parent or guardian (e.g., parent education courses, family counseling)
  - Detention or probation
  - Counseling
  - Drug testing
  - Dropout prevention or other courses

This primarily reactive and punitive approach has been used by schools for decades despite limited positive effects. Truancy court may be an effective last step for a very small number of students; however, this step should occur only when significant preventive and less intensive intervention efforts have been tried and found unsuccessful. We use the analogy that truancy court is like heart bypass surgery for someone with severely blocked or damaged arteries. It is a last-stage effort used only in the most extreme cases where many other less costly, less complicated, and less risky preventive measures have already been tried. We need to begin to shift our model from a reliance on reactive and punitive approaches to those that are preventive and positive in focus and that use proven principles of behavioral change.

Toward a New Model

Within the field of education, we have acquired a host of information about best practices for changing student behavior. The Safe & Civil Schools model of absenteeism prevention and intervention takes what we already know about changing any problematic behavior (e.g., disruptive or defiant behavior) and applies it to address absenteeism. Some of the key components of this model include:

- A belief that behavior can be changed
- An increased focus on prevention and proactive measures (e.g., using evidence-based approaches, such as positive behavioral interventions and supports [PBIS] and multi-tiered systems of support [MTSS])
- A common definition and language related to attendance. Here's a preview of essential metrics to monitor and address that will be discussed in more detail in subsequent chapters:

Essential Metrics

Calculate the following metrics using a combination of unexcused absences, excused absences, and suspensions:

Regular Attendance: Absent 5 percent or less (the goal for all students)

Chronic Absence: Absent 10 percent or more

- An understanding that we need to monitor the data and intervene as early as possible when a problem begins to emerge
- An understanding that our efforts should attempt, as much as possible, to address the causes of the problematic behavior

A few other guiding principles include:

- Schools should work to address all types of absenteeism, including excused, unexcused, and suspension-related absences.
- Because teachers are the school personnel who have the closest relationship with students and families, they play a primary role in building a culture of attendance.
- All stakeholders have a role to play in efforts to address absenteeism—including administrators, teachers, paraprofessionals, other classified and certified staff, students, families, and even community members.
- We cannot punish students into wanting to attend school!

How to Use This Book

Teacher's Guide to Tackling Attendance Challenges is designed to give classroom teachers the information and resources needed to build a strong classroom-based initiative to improve the attendance of all students. This initiative can be done on your own or in partnership with other teachers in your school. The book provides an overarching framework for implementation, as well as lesson plan samples, examples and reproducibles for reinforcement systems, and talking points for use with students and families. We also include many real-world examples of successful classroom-based approaches and stories of the differences these approaches have made for teachers and students.

This book can also be used in conjunction with the companion resource—*School Leader's Guide to Tackling Attendance Challenges.* If a school or district is interested in a comprehensive approach to address absenteeism across classrooms, *School Leader's Guide* covers all aspects of implementing a systematic, multi-tiered approach to absenteeism prevention and intervention. Designed for use with school-based teams such as PBIS teams, leadership teams, and attendance teams or task forces, *School Leader's Guide* can also be used by district and building administrators, school board members, and other policymakers who seek to improve attendance, address academic achievement, and/or increase funding. When used together, *School Leader's Guide to Tackling Attendance Challenges* provides guidance for implementing a multi-tiered schoolwide approach and *Teacher's Guide to Tackling Attendance Challenges* provides significantly expanded examples of lesson plans and other practical classroom resources.

K–12 Applications

The overarching procedures in this book are applicable across grades K–12. While we have made efforts to provide examples and samples across all these grade levels, additional focus is placed on early intervention in primary and elementary grades, as well as the middle school transition. When absenteeism problems in elementary school or early middle school are not addressed, additional related problems can occur in later middle and high school, when prevention and intervention with absenteeism become more complex. What may be a simple problem in elementary school, such as lack of understanding about the importance of attendance or lack of reliable transportation, may lead to a host of other problems if left unaddressed, such as the student falling behind academically or disengaging from adults or peers. The longer the problem goes on, the more complex, difficult, and resource-intensive the intervention becomes. This resource will provide ongoing emphasis on the importance of starting the work of building a culture of attendance as early as prekindergarten and kindergarten.

Addressing Tardies

The approaches described in this book are easily modified to address excessive morning tardies (e.g., when large numbers of students arrive up to 30 minutes to an hour late in the morning) or excessive end-of-day absences (e.g., when large numbers of students are picked up from school prior to the end of the school day). If these kinds of tardies or time-of-day absences are problematic for large numbers of students in your school, consider how strategies such as educating students and families, motivational systems, and other universal classroom systems described in Chapters 2–5 can be modified to address the problem. If individual students struggle with tardiness, see the strategies in Chapter 6 for early-stage intervention approaches and suggestions for connecting the student with intervention resources outside the classroom.

In secondary schools, if excessive tardies occur in many classrooms throughout the day after each passing period, your school might consider implementing *START on Time!* This program helps middle and high school administrators and staff improve student behavior in hallways and reduce the frequency of tardiness by over 90 percent. *START on Time!* includes a manual and video presentations, and is available from Ancora Publishing (ancorapublishing.com).

■ ■ ■ ■ ■

For far too long, attendance has been viewed as something beyond our control: "It's a parent problem" or "She's just unmotivated, so there's really nothing we can do to make her come to school." However, emerging research and the experiences we've had working with schools to implement positive and proactive approaches to absenteeism issues have shown us that this issue is far from beyond our control. In fact, teachers have great power to effect positive change. When you actively work to create a culture of attendance in your classroom, the impact on your students and the overall functioning of your classroom can be immense. Let's get started!

1

Attendance—Not Another Competing Initiative

If you picked up this book on your own, you are probably already motivated to tackle absenteeism problems (or you just geek out on educational books like we do!). However, if your school or district asked you to read this book and implement the strategies within, you may be skeptical about why you should address chronic absence when faced with so many other pressing challenges, like defiant behavior or students failing courses and state tests. Teachers are faced with an incredible number of responsibilities and competing initiatives and priorities, so we need to ensure that our time is used wisely. This chapter answers the crucial question, "Why should I spend my time addressing chronic absence?" We hope that the research and other rationales provided get you excited to tackle attendance. Improving attendance can positively affect other academic and behavioral initiatives, so this work should not be viewed as a competing initiative. Rather, this complementary initiative will enhance other work you are already doing, with students more consistently present to participate in academic instruction and other class and school opportunities. We hope that you leave this chapter with the knowledge that your efforts to build a classroom culture of attendance will significantly improve student outcomes, your classroom, and your personal job satisfaction.

This chapter briefly summarizes current findings on the prevalence and trends in rates of chronic absence. It also provides information on the negative effects of absenteeism that are supported by research and that we have heard repeatedly from educators around the country. These negative effects occur for the student, the class and school, the families, the community, and society. Skim this chapter for a broad overview and confirmation of why it is important to invest your efforts in addressing absenteeism. You may want to return to this content when you work through Chapters 4 and 5 ("If You Want It, Teach It!" and "Partnering with Families") as you determine what information to share with students and families.

We provide citations for relevant research in this book in case they may be useful in advocating for a schoolwide or district initiative. You can also find more detailed descriptions of the findings related to prevalence and negative effects of absenteeism in Chapter 1 of this book's companion resource, *School Leader's Guide to Tackling Attendance Challenges.*

Prevalence of Chronic Absence Across the Nation

The U.S. Office for Civil Rights data set from 2013–2014 was the first to report nationwide absence rates. The data indicated that approximately 14 percent of the student population—over 6.5 million students—missed 15 days or more of school. While this threshold is slightly lower than the 18 days of absence (10 percent) across a traditional 180-day school year that is typically used to identify chronic absentees, it clearly indicates that far too many students are missing critical amounts of school. These data are also similar to previous estimates that 10 percent to 15 percent of students were chronically absent nationwide (Balfanz & Byrnes, 2012).

While absenteeism is widespread across the United States, certain districts and schools clearly experience increased rates of absenteeism.

> While some schools may have chronic absence rates below five percent of their student body, in 2013–2014, 500 school districts nationwide reported that 30 percent or more of their student body missed 15 or more days of school or more. Far too many students are missing critical amounts of school.

Though most researchers are careful not to definitively attribute a cause to this variability, the rate of poverty is the variable most strongly associated with levels of chronic absence. Districts and schools with higher rates of poverty, regardless of other demographics (e.g., urban, suburban, rural, race/ethnicity), are likely to experience higher rates of chronic absence (Attendance Works and the Everyone Graduates Center, 2017; Balfanz & Byrnes, 2012; Ginsberg, Chang, & Jordan, 2014). For example, in Utah, students from low-income homes (who received free and reduced-price lunch) were 90 percent more likely to be chronically absent than students who were not from low-income homes (Utah Education Policy Center, 2012). When you consider the additional challenges that may be faced by students living in poverty (e.g., lack of reliable transportation or clean clothes, food insecurity, housing instability), the relationship between poverty and an increased likelihood of chronic absence is unsurprising. Two of the most prominent researchers in this field conclude that one of the most effective ways to help students out of situations of poverty is to get them to attend school each day (Balfanz & Byrnes, 2012).

Additional trends to be aware of include:

- Absenteeism is problematic for many students in kindergarten and 1st grade.
- Absenteeism increases throughout middle and high school.
- Chronic absenteeism is more prevalent for specific minority groups (e.g., American Indian and Alaska Native students exhibit higher rates of absenteeism across grades than Asian or white students).
- Chronic absenteeism is more prevalent for students with disabilities.
- Students who are highly mobile (foster children, children whose parents do migratory work, students who are homeless) are some of the students most likely to have problematic attendance.

(Balfanz & Byrnes, 2012; Romero & Lee, 2007; U.S. Dept. of Education Office for Civil Rights, 2016; Utah Education Policy Center, University of Utah, 2012).

Brainstorming the Negative Impacts of Chronic Absence

Before you read the following sections on how attendance negatively affects students, classrooms, families, and communities, we encourage you to take a moment to brainstorm the negative effects of chronic absence on your own classroom and students.

In facilitating trainings across the country, we find that most educators have already thought about some of the negative academic impacts that can occur for individual students. However, they may not have deeply considered the ripple effects that can occur in all parts of schools and beyond. Think about your students and what you have seen in your classes. Figure 1.1 presents a chart that can be used to brainstorm the possible negative effects of absenteeism for students both inside and outside of school (column 1); the class—the teacher and other students—and school (column 2); and the broader community—parents, community, and society (column 3). Afterward, read the remainder of the chapter for a discussion of the negative effects highlighted from the research and testimonials from other educators.

FIGURE 1.1 **Brainstorming Negative Effects of Absenteeism**

For the Student	For the Class/School	For Parents/Families/ Community/Society
Inside school: Outside school:	The teacher: Other students: The school:	Parents/families: Local community: Society:

How Irregular Attendance Negatively Impacts Students

Negative Academic Outcomes

Students who are frequently absent from school are more likely to experience negative academic outcomes. Even as early as kindergarten, students who miss 10 percent or more of the school year score lower than their peers on reading, math, and general knowledge measures (Romero & Lee, 2007). All families should receive information as soon as their child enters kindergarten about the essential basic skills their child will learn in kindergarten. This information should emphasize that regular and repeated practice of skills like phonemic awareness, phonics, and vocabulary in reading and one-to-one number correspondence in math are critical to setting up students for success. Even sporadic absences can cause their child to fall behind. If you work with kindergarten or 1st-grade students, you may need to make the effort to help families understand that their children are no longer attending day care and that ensuring regular attendance is one of the best things they can do to put their children on a track for success.

Rethinking Kindergarten Vacation

A few years ago, I went to speak at a conference near Disneyland in February. My kids were one and three at the time. We decided to add a family vacation to the conference travel because Disneyland would be relatively uncrowded midweek during February. We had a wonderful time and had very few lines to stand in. I remember thinking, "Maybe we can do this every other year and make it a tradition." Then I remembered that my son would be in kindergarten in two years. I was presenting at the conference on improving attendance and had just spoken to a group of educators about the importance of consistent kindergarten attendance, and here I was thinking about taking my son out for a week for Disneyland! I realized it wouldn't be the right thing to do, even if it would be nice to beat the crowds in the off-season. We would just have to brave the lines during the summer or another school vacation time!

—Jessica Sprick

A few other academic trends to be aware of include:

- Early absenteeism predicts later absenteeism (Buehler, Tapogna, & Chang, 2012; Connolly & Olson, 2012; Ehrlich, Gwynne, Pareja, & Allensworth, 2013), and each successive year of chronic absenteeism is related to significant and compounded risk of reduced learning (Chang & Romero, 2008; Easton & Englehard, 1982; Erlich et al., 2013).

- As students progress through school, those who are chronically absent have consistently lower GPAs and test scores (Barge, 2011; Ginsberg et al., 2014; Gottfried, 2010).
- Students with high levels of absenteeism are at greater risk for dropping out than their peers with regular attendance, and absenteeism is predictive of dropout beginning as early as 1st grade (Alexander, Entwisle, & Horsey, 1997; Balfanz & Byrnes, 2012; Balfanz, Herzog, & Mac Iver, 2007; Hammond, Linton, Smink, & Drew, 2007; Neild, Balfanz, & Herzog, 2007; Rumberger & Thomas, 2000).

Exacerbation of Social-Emotional Problems

When students fall behind in their classes due to absenteeism, this can lead to a dangerous pattern of increased frustration, negative behavior, and exclusion. Picture the following vicious cycle: A student acts out due to frustration with academic or social difficulties in classes. If it is serious, this behavior causes the student to be excluded from class and school activities. For many students, while they are out of school, they are not being taught the replacement behaviors or skills that will help them be more successful in the classroom. The student's absence leads to further frustration upon the student's return to class or school, which can then perpetuate the cycle of exclusion.

When Johnny Is Absent, It's So Quiet!

We frequently hear educators say things like, "Have you noticed that the students with behavioral issues are the ones who are *always* in school?" This is often said somewhat wistfully, as teachers think about how quiet and orderly things would be if those students were absent a little more often. However, we want to discuss two important concepts that are embedded within this statement: 1) some students with behavioral issues attend school every day because school is a safe haven from other, more difficult aspects of their lives, and 2) while you may breathe a small and natural sigh of relief on days when students with behavioral issues are absent, remember that they always come back! When students return from an absence, they are typically a little further behind and a little more disconnected from school, which can in turn increase behavioral issues. With these two important concepts in mind, teachers have to work doubly hard to try to make sure that students with behavioral issues are in class every day. It's also the only way to ensure they are receiving the necessary behavioral instruction, practice, and interventions necessary to help them learn more adaptive and prosocial behaviors!

—Jessica Sprick and Tricia Berg

Students who are frequently absent may find it difficult to build meaningful connections with staff members and other students, and they may struggle to develop the behavioral and social-emotional skills needed to be successful in school and in life. When students are absent to avoid aversive situations at school—such as conflict with peers or staff, bullying situations, academic difficulties, or other uncomfortable interactions—they may not develop conflict resolution, resilience, and self-advocacy skills. They will learn over time to simply avoid uncomfortable situations by withdrawing and not showing up. Research also suggests that students who are chronically absent face increased alienation from classmates and peers (Gottfried, 2014; Reid, 1981). Friendships may shift when the student is frequently absent, as the student's friends seek peers who are more consistently available. Peers may also resent picking up the slack for students who are absent when there is a group project or partner work or helping absent students catch up when they return to school.

Negative Behaviors and Activities Outside of School

Students who are chronically absent have higher rates of involvement in delinquent and other risk-taking behavior, such as drugs and alcohol, early sexual experiences, and gang activity (Dalun et al., 2010; Dryfoos, 1990; Farrington, 1996; Garry, 1996; Hallfors et al., 2002; Henry & Huizinga, 2007; Loeber & Farrington, 2000). They are also far more likely to experience negative outcomes later in life, such as involvement in the criminal justice system, poorer mental health outcomes, lower-paying jobs, and an increased likelihood of unemployment (Alexander et al., 1997; Hibbett, Fogelman, & Manor, 1990; Kane, 2006; Robins & Ratcliff, 1980; Rocque, Jennings, Piquero, Ozkan, & Farrington, 2017).

One of the greatest concerns with chronic absence that persists into high school is that students do not develop the habits of being present and showing up on time every day. Most employers indicate that dependability (showing up on time every day when not seriously ill) is one of the most important factors in maintaining a job, and in some ways it matters more than a person's natural talent. A lack of dependability can lead to serious negative outcomes, such as a lack of promotion despite one's talents and abilities or even being fired. For example, a high school principal in Oregon told us that he tracked the job performance and attendance of recent graduates who entered the local job force. He found that students who had problematic attendance in high school continued to have problematic attendance in their jobs and had difficulty maintaining employment.

How Irregular Attendance Negatively Impacts the Class

Effects on Teachers

We know how valuable every minute of instructional time is for you and your students, and that each moment of your prep time is precious. So, when students are absent and parents say, "Send home makeup work, and we will make sure she gets caught up," we know that it is not always that simple! Makeup work requires significant time and effort to prepare if it is to provide a somewhat adequate level of instruction to make up for the missed class activities. You also have to put in extra effort to track different due dates for makeup work and ensure that the student is making sufficient progress after an absence. This is time that could be spent planning meaningful classroom activities.

In cases where students and parents are not willing or able to get the student caught up outside the class, you will need to spend class time catching absent students up to the rest of the class. In fact, numerous studies have found that when students are chronically absent, it slows down instruction for all students, and a significant amount of instructional time is lost (Blazer, 2011; Chang & Jordan, 2011; Musser, 2011; Nauer, White, & Yerneni, 2008). If students who are chronically absent exhibit increased disruptive behavior as they grow frustrated, you will need to spend more time on behavior management, detracting from time to serve other students who regularly attend school.

Effects on Other Students

Instructional activities may become significantly more difficult when students are frequently absent. We cannot overstate the importance of building a trusting class community in order to facilitate learning. Because learning requires people to be vulnerable and admit to themselves and others that they do not know everything, a certain level of comfort and trust with peers and adults in the learning environment is required. When students are frequently absent, it is difficult to build this kind of trusting community. Students may be reluctant to be vulnerable, make mistakes, and attempt to learn. In classes that use partner and group activities, absences cause numerous difficulties. It may be a struggle to place the peers of absent students into new partnerships or groups without a loss of instructional time. You may also experience difficulties with classroom climate, such as peers who resent having to take over work for their absent classmate or struggles to maintain instructional momentum with groups.

We have heard educators frequently express concerns that peers observe the absenteeism of their classmates and worry about why their friends are absent. In other cases, peers begin to question why they need to attend when they see that their friends are frequently absent. This leads to a general devaluing of school and the importance of attendance. Many educators express concerns that absenteeism can be contagious—the more some students are absent, the more their peers will also decide that attendance is not necessary.

How Irregular Attendance Negatively Impacts Parents and Families, Communities, and Society

Effects on Parents and Families

For many parents, taking off work when their child is absent or suspended from school is simply not an option, or they may experience significantly increased stress as they attempt to adjust their schedule or find care for the student who is not in school. They may need to scramble to find an alternative caregiver, or in the worst-case scenario, simply leave their child unsupervised during an excused absence or suspension. Each of these situations can cause hardship on the family, especially when absences are frequent. When a student is absent due to suspension, the relationship between parents and school staff can become adversarial. Parents may wish to support the school but are frustrated by the school's inability to handle school-based problems at school. They may also be concerned about possible ramifications to their jobs and feel the school is placing an undue burden on them by suspending the student from school.

Effects on Local Communities and Society

When students have excessive absenteeism, communities and society pay the price—via student delinquency and lack of job preparedness. Because high rates of absenteeism are strongly related to students dropping out of school, any negative effects of dropout on communities and society can be associated with chronic absence as well. The estimated economic consequences of dropping out of school are immense—averaging close to $240,000 per dropout—resulting from lower tax contributions, greater reliance on government programs and assistance, and higher rates of criminal activity (Levin & Belfield 2007; Maynard, Salas-Wright, & Vaughn, 2015; Rouse, 2007). Chronic absence is linked to crime and delinquency, and students who are chronically absent are more likely to use drugs and alcohol, have early sexual experiences, and engage in gang activity (Dalun et al., 2010; Dryfoos, 1990; Farrington, 1996; Garry, 1996; Hallfors et al., 2002; Henry & Huizinga, 2007; Loeber & Farrington, 2000). Because students are also less likely to develop necessary habits and attitudes for job performance, they are more likely to place a burden on their communities later in life as they struggle to acquire and maintain a job.

■ ■ ■ ■ ■

Student attendance has wide-reaching implications for students, classes, and communities. In this chapter, we provided summaries of research on the prevalence of absenteeism in schools and the resulting negative effects. We also shared negative effects that, while not yet supported by research, were recounted to us by countless educators around the country as we worked with them to tackle attendance issues in their schools. This chapter provides the rationale and foundation on which to base your attendance initiative. The remaining chapters in this book will provide strategies and examples of how you can change the culture of attendance in your classroom.

2

Gathering and Analyzing the Right Data

We believe that good work in schools starts with good data. Jake Alabiso, a school psychologist at Barnes Elementary, one of the schools that we have had the great privilege to work with, said the following about the importance of data at the start of their attendance initiative:

> For years, the staff knew we had an "attendance problem," but we failed to address the issue systematically. The reasons for this were threefold: 1) a lack of knowledge, 2) a mistaken belief that effecting meaningful change was not possible for what we thought to be primarily a home-based problem, and 3) the lack of accessible data. We plugged along for years, with individual teachers and our attendance clerk occasionally lamenting our attendance issues, but never developing any momentum to tackle the problem.
>
> In March 2014, all this changed. We attended a conference where several of our PBIS team members attended a Safe & Civil Schools presentation on attendance. It struck a very strong chord with our team. They walked away

> armed with new vocabulary, data, research and, most importantly, hope that we could improve our schoolwide attendance rate. The "aha" moment came when the teachers roughly tabulated attendance data for their individual classrooms. They were completely blown away by how much school their students were missing.

Jake reported that the teaching staff all became highly motivated to tackle the issue of chronic absence once they broke down the data for their own students. The teachers' motivation was a huge factor in the success Barnes Elementary had tackling chronic absenteeism. This story emphasizes the importance of good data when tackling any classroom or schoolwide issue. In order to intervene effectively, you first have to identify that there is a problem. Then you must determine its magnitude and potential causes before an effective plan of action can be put in place. This all requires data. However, collecting data must not become so onerous that it is discouraging. In this chapter, we provide clarity on definitions and simple methods for collecting and analyzing attendance data in your classroom so you can identify classroom trends, as well as individual students who require support. This chapter also provides suggestions for teacher-led problem-solving processes that can be used to address whole-class attendance issues or individual student difficulties with attendance.

Note

The procedures in this chapter all describe data collection systems you can use in your own classroom. However, if your school or district is working on an attendance campaign, school or district attendance clerks may be able to provide data reports from the school information system. It may also be possible to pull reports directly from your attendance information system. If your attendance clerk is not familiar with how to compile the recommended reports, ask your administrator if you can contact the information system operators to request information on how to gather the necessary data.

Understand Commonly Used Metrics

Most schools collect data on *truancy* and *average daily attendance*. While these data are useful, it is important to recognize that relying on them alone can be misleading as to the extent of absenteeism problems in a school.

Truancy typically describes absences that occur without parent permission. It is important to recognize that unexcused absences are not the only problematic type of absences. Warning systems that look only at truancy will often fail to catch a large number of students who exhibit problematic patterns of attendance, especially those that occur in elementary school, where the majority of absences are excused. Consider the following as an example of what can occur when you look only at truancy data.

Jeremiah was a 7th grader who was referred for Tier 3 supports due to significant course failure across all his classes. When our intervention team examined his course records, it quickly became clear that he had patterns of excessive absenteeism (e.g., averaging approximately one to two days of absence a week), but his attendance was never flagged as a problem because the school was looking at truancy and all of Jeremiah's absences were excused. This pattern of chronic absences had started in early elementary school, but because the absences were excused, they were never addressed as problematic. He was triggered as needing support only when his course failure reflected the fact that he was often out of class, and this course failure flagged the attention of staff. As the team worked to intervene to address Jeremiah's course failure, one of the first things we knew we had to tackle was the pattern of severe chronic absence, which had to start with getting his mom on board. Jeremiah would complain of colds and headaches to get out of coming to school, so we helped his mom implement a plan that required a doctor's visit or approval from the school nurse before she would allow him to stay home. As Jeremiah's attendance improved, we worked to address other issues, such as anxiety, that were contributing to Jeremiah's not wanting to come to school. As a result, his work completion, test scores, and grades also improved.

Average daily attendance (ADA) is tracked in many schools, and in some states ADA is a partial funding mechanism (i.e., the higher the ADA, the more funding the school receives). ADA is a measure of the average percentage of students in the student body who are present each day across the course of the school year. If a class or school has a 92 percent ADA, this means that an average of 92 percent of the students are present each day. As a whole-class or whole-school measure, ADA can be useful for getting a broad picture of the overall rate of attendance, and it can be used to set group goals for improvement (e.g., "We had an ADA of 92 percent last month—let's strive for 94 percent this month!"). However, ADA provides no information about individual students whose attendance contributes positively or negatively to the whole-school percentage. Even a class with a 95 percent ADA, which is often viewed as a good ADA rate, may have large numbers of students highly at risk due to problematic attendance. This can occur when the majority of students have very good attendance and a smaller, but still significant, number of students have poor attendance.

Consider evaluating truancy and ADA data in conjunction with individualized metrics.

Understand Individualized Metrics

In the last 20 years, researchers and school professionals have attempted to determine critical thresholds, or red flags, at which a student's absenteeism can be viewed as highly problematic and a likely route to school failure and dropout. The following individualized metrics have emerged as critical indicators: regular attendance, at-risk attendance, chronic absence, and severe chronic absence. (*Note:* Chronic absence and regular attendance are described first because chronic absence is the critical red flag for intervention, and regular attendance is the goal for every student.)

Chronic Absence

Chronic absence is defined as missing 10 percent or more of school for any reason, including unexcused absences, excused absences, and suspensions. (*Note:* In some schools, suspensions are considered excused absences and thus are also included when a district or school defines chronic absence as a measure of excused and unexcused absences.)

This metric has emerged as the point at which absenteeism is strongly associated with negative outcomes, such as course failure and dropout. In 2010, Sparks summarized the emerging research trends, stating, "A growing consensus of research points to chronic absence . . . as one of the strongest and most overlooked indicators of a student's risk of become disengaged, failing courses, and eventually dropping out of school" (p. 1). Since that time, an exponential increase in chronic absenteeism research points to a relationship between chronic absence and negative student outcomes. Therefore, this resource, along with a growing number of education experts, state Departments of Education, and federal sources, recommends analyzing chronic absence data and using this metric as a measure of school effectiveness.

At the outset of our work at Safe & Civil Schools to help schools tackle absenteeism, the metric of chronic absence was relatively new and largely unknown to most teachers and other educational professionals. These educators often attended professional development programs on attendance focused on looking for strategies to intervene with those few students who had 60, 90, or 100+ days of absence. However, when we explained that students who miss only 10 percent of days (approximately 18 days in most school systems) are highly at risk, many educators were shocked when they realized the high percentage of students in their classes or schools who were now categorized as at risk. While expanding the risk pool with the metric of chronic absence may make the task of addressing absenteeism more daunting, it also creates a more accurate picture of how attendance may be positively or negatively affecting each school, class, and individual student. This can help educators determine how much time and energy to place on improving student attendance through the preventive and early intervention measures described in this book.

Regular Attendance

Regular attendance, as related to chronic absence, is defined as missing 5 percent or less of school for any reason, including unexcused absences, excused absences, and suspension. Just as chronic absence is viewed as a critical point at which negative effects are likely, regular attendance is a critical point at which a school may assume that a student is unlikely to suffer negative effects related to absenteeism. If a student has regular attendance (missing no more than 5 percent of school days) but exhibits signs of disengagement, academic failure, or other concerns, the school can likely rule out absenteeism as the cause of these negative patterns. The goal for a school's attendance efforts is that every student regularly attend school, missing no more than 5 percent of days in the school year.

At-Risk Attendance

In between regular attendance and chronic absence is *at-risk attendance* (missing 5.1 percent to 9.9 percent of school), whereby a student may or may not suffer negative effects of absenteeism but should be carefully monitored. For students in the at-risk category, implement universal preventive measures and early-stage interventions to try to prevent further problems with absenteeism.

Severe Chronic Absence

Severe chronic absence, defined as missing 20 percent or more of school, can be viewed as a highly intensive level of absenteeism that warrants immediate intervention. Without support and intervention, most students in this category are on a predictable path toward school failure.

Individualized Metrics Within a Continuum

While, for the sake of clarity, the categories of regular, at-risk, chronic, and severe chronic are defined according to a specific percentage of days present or absent, we recommend thinking about students' attendance as a continuum that has increasing levels of risk with increasing levels of absenteeism (see Figure 2.1). In reality, there is little difference between a student who has missed 9.5 percent of the school year and a student who has missed 10 percent. Both students may need similar levels of support, even though one is defined as at risk and the other is in the chronic absence category.

FIGURE 2.1 **Increased Levels of Absenteeism Lead to Increased Levels of Risk**

Severe Chronic Absence

20% or more

Chronic Absence

10%–19.9%

At-Risk Attendance

5.1%–9.9%

Regular Attendance

5% or less

Conceptualize Percentages Versus Number of Days

A percentage, rather than number of days, is used in the definition of chronic absenteeism to ensure that educators do not wait to intervene until a student has reached a certain number of days absent (e.g., 10 days or 18 days). Using percentages ensures that whenever data are analyzed during the school year, you can identify students who are chronically absent, at risk, and regularly present at that particular point in the year. For example, a student would be considered chronically absent across the whole school year when he misses 10 percent of days, or 18 days in a 180-day school year. However, you should not wait until the end of the year to determine that this student has a problematic attendance rate. If the student misses 10 percent in the first 20 days (i.e., misses two or more days), intervention may be warranted. At the least, you should carefully observe the student's attendance across the next 20 days. What is important to remember is that if the student misses an average of two or more days a month according to a typical school calendar (180 days), he is considered chronically absent. If your school operates on a different school calendar (e.g., four-day weeks or a shortened or lengthened school year), calculate the attendance percentages accordingly.

Also, remember and emphasize the goal—that *every* student is regularly present (missing no more than 5 percent of days). This means that each student should miss no more than an average of one day per month in a typical 180-day school year.

THE GOAL

Every student is regularly present. This means each student should miss no more than an average of one day per month.

Record Accurate and Timely Attendance Data

The key to having usable, useful attendance data is to accurately record attendance each day! We know how difficult it can be to make this happen as you strive to create an engaging start to classroom instruction each day or period, students come in late, or there are other interruptions to instruction. However, recording accurate attendance data in a timely manner is one of the only nonnegotiables that you will find in this book because of the serious safety implications when a staff member forgets or chooses not to take attendance. Imagine the following scenario: A parent unexpectedly calls or comes to school because of a family emergency. The attendance report indicates that the student is in class, or the school finds that attendance has not been reported for the student's class. When school staff go to collect the student, they find that the student is not in the classroom, and they now have to inform the parent that they do not know where the student is. Schools are responsible for the safety of their students during school hours, so this scenario should never be a reality. We have heard horrifying stories about students who have run away from home or been abducted and no one knew about it for a whole day because the school did not accurately record and monitor student attendance. The following suggestions may help make taking attendance less onerous. If you are already doing these or similar things, you should be able to quickly skim through the following suggestions. On the other hand, if your current procedures take too long and students become restless, or if you simply lose valuable instructional time as you take attendance, consider incorporating some or all of these suggestions.

Use Assigned Seats

Roll call is the antithesis of an engaging start to a class. Remember the attendance roll call in *Ferris Bueller's Day Off*: "Bueller . . . Bueller . . . Bueller . . ."? Assigning seats has many benefits (e.g., reducing management problems, creating intentional instructional pairings), but one of the biggest is that it allows you to eliminate roll call. With assigned seats, you can quickly glance at which students are present and which are absent. If your students are highly motivated and well behaved, you may want to have them write the names of three to five students they would like to sit next to (as opposed to letting students pick who they would like to sit next to, which can be demotivating for students with no friends) and create an assigned-seating chart that accommodates as many student requests as possible. You can tell students who did not get to sit next to a requested peer in the first seating chart that you will pair them with one of their requests in the next seating chart a few weeks later.

Another benefit of an assigned-seating chart is the support it gives to substitutes. When students are in their assigned seats, take a picture of each group of desks or each row, or attach student photos next to their names on the assigned-seating chart. Substitutes will be able to see that students are actually sitting in their assigned seats, not in another seat pretending to be someone else to be near a friend. This can prevent many behavior management issues that occur when substitutes are present, in addition to helping ensure that you have accurate attendance records and that the school knows, for safety reasons, who is present and who is absent.

Use Efficient Start-of-Class Routines

The easiest way to make sure you enter roll regularly is to establish a routine that involves a warm-up or entry task within the first five or 10 minutes of class. While students are completing the one- to two-minute silent warm-up task at their seats, you can use the assigned-seating chart to enter class attendance into your attendance system and classroom attendance charts. (*Note:* Classroom attendance charts are discussed later in this chapter.) Students remain instructionally engaged while you take and enter attendance.

Another possibility is to create an "attendance entry" or "attendance delivery" job. Have a reliable student use the assigned-seating chart to identify students who are absent and give those names to you so you can enter them into the attendance system. In some cases, it may be appropriate for the student to enter the information into the attendance system without submitting it (the teacher should always double-check and then submit). Or the student might hand-deliver the attendance sheet to the office.

Finally, ensure that you have efficient processes for recording tardies and updating the attendance record when students come in late. Nothing is more disruptive than stopping instruction each time a student enters the class late so that you can get information about the reason for the late arrival and adjust the attendance record. Procedures for dealing with tardiness should keep students who come in late from disrupting the flow of instruction, and they should also ensure that you have an accurate record of how many tardies each student has, both excused and unexcused. The CHAMPS recommendations for classroom tardy procedures presented are those from *CHAMPS: A Proactive and Positive Approach to Classroom Management.*

Set a Reminder Alarm on your Phone or Watch

The CHAMPS recommendations help you follow a regular process for recording attendance. However, interruptions naturally happen that can disrupt your routines and leave gaps in your attendance record. Set a recurring alarm on your phone, watch, or other device that will give you a reminder 10 minutes into the class period to update your attendance if you have not already done so. This kind of backup system is especially important if you regularly struggle to turn in attendance. While some schools have procedures to provide reminders to all teachers (e.g., teacher assistants in the front office who run reminder slips to teachers who have not submitted attendance), if this schoolwide support is not available to you, find ways to provide personal prompts and reminders to yourself.

CHAMPS Recommendations for Classroom Tardy Procedures

One effective procedure for dealing with tardy students is to have a three-ring binder filled with forms similar to this Record of Tardies.

Record of Tardies

Teacher: ____________________ Date: __________

Names	Excused	Unexcused
	❑	❑
1st Period	❑	❑
	❑	❑
	❑	❑
2nd Period	❑	❑
	❑	❑
	❑	❑
3rd Period	❑	❑
	❑	❑
	❑	❑
4th Period	❑	❑
	❑	❑
	❑	❑
5th Period	❑	❑
	❑	❑
	❑	❑
6th Period	❑	❑
	❑	❑
	❑	❑
7th Period	❑	❑
	❑	❑

Place the binder on a table or shelf near the door to the classroom. Each day before students arrive, make sure that a new page is showing with the correct day and date filled in at the top. Attach a few paper clips to the page so that students who have excused tardies can attach either the excuse slip from the attendance office or a note from the teacher who is excusing the tardy.

Prior to using this system, teach your students the procedure they will follow when tardy, whether it is excused or unexcused. Tell them they are to quietly enter the classroom without interrupting you or any other student. They will go to the tardy notebook, write their names in the box for the appropriate period, indicate excused or unexcused, and attach the excuse slip if they have one. Then they should quietly go to their seats and join class activities.

When a student enters late, do not stop what you are doing or verbally acknowledge the student. Visually monitor that the student goes to the notebook and writes something (you can check later to make sure the student filled in the form appropriately). If the student does not go to the notebook, provide a verbal reminder, "Paul, before you sit down, put your name in the tardy notebook and indicate whether it is excused or unexcused. Now, class, what I was saying was . . ."

As soon as possible during the period, when the class is engaged with independent or cooperative group work, check the information in the notebook. Record the tardy in your attendance record or grade book and follow any procedures for reporting unexcused tardies to the attendance office. If your school automatically calls home when students are reported absent, ensure that notification of the student's tardy is sent to the office as soon as the student arrives to class. This would be an appropriate job for a highly responsible student who could call the attendance clerk or run a slip to the office indicating the student has arrived.

If you need to talk to a student about being tardy, ensure that this discussion occurs when the rest of the class is instructionally engaged. All your procedures should prevent tardy student(s) from getting attention and interrupting your lesson. If you notice a pattern of tardies with an individual student, consider adapting one or more interventions described in Chapter 6. If tardiness is a problem for many students in your class, consider adapting one or more of the whole-class procedures (e.g., lessons, motivational systems, communication with families) described in Chapters 3–5 of this book, and work with your

(continued)

school to explore ways of implementing whole-school prevention when the problem is pervasive across classes (e.g., Safe & Civil Schools' *START on Time!* for secondary schools).

Source: From *CHAMPS: A Proactive and Positive Approach to Classroom Management*, by R. Sprick, 2009, Eugene, OR: Ancora Publishing. Copyright 2009 by Ancora Publishing. Adapted with permission.

Monitor Classroom Attendance Across Time

As you take attendance, select an easy and efficient way to keep a classroom record of which students were absent and when. The goal is to monitor over time how many absences each student accumulates. We recommend analyzing the data every 20 days (approximately once a month) to see which students were chronically absent during the month (e.g., the student missed two or more days out of 20 days of school). Also, use the data to determine every student's cumulative attendance rate for the year (i.e., the number of days the student has been absent since the start of the school year).

If your data system allows you to obtain a report that shows the attendance rate for each individual student in your class (without requiring you to pull the record for each student separately), you may not need to use a manual method, like the following one. However, mark on your calendar the dates when you will pull the data from the attendance system. We recommend obtaining the data at least once a month, especially if you know that chronic absence is a significant problem in your class. If your data system does not allow you to easily determine the attendance rate for each student in the class, or you prefer to use a manual method, consider the following procedure.

Keep a Monthly Classroom Record of Attendance

Design a chart (see Figure 2.2) with 20 days so you can mark students' attendance each day at the same time you update the school attendance record. Mark an X for any absence. At the end of the 20-day period, add up the absences for each student and determine each student's attendance category for the 20 days. For example, in 20 days, any students with no absences are in the regular attendance category, students with one absence fall in the at-risk category, students with two to three days fall in the chronic absence category, and students with four or more days fall in the severe chronic absence

FIGURE 2.2 **Sample Classroom Record of Attendance**

October Attendance Record (5th Period) Regular attendance = 0 days, at risk = 1 day, chronic absence = 2–3 days, severe chronic absence = 4+ days

Name	2-Oct	3-Oct	4-Oct	5-Oct	6-Oct	10-Oct	11-Oct	12-Oct	13-Oct	16-Oct	17-Oct	18-Oct	19-Oct	20-Oct	23-Oct	24-Oct	25-Oct	26-Oct	27-Oct	30-Oct	Total Days = 20
Martin Anderson		X	X				X									X					4
Selah Artiz																					0
Dante Bjorquist													X								1
Joseph Chen																					0
Monique Collins				X	X																2
Jacob Edwards													X								1
Simone Everett				X																	1
Ivy Farrows																					0
Duncan Hines																					0
Kayaba Iddrisu										X											1
Jordan Jones										X										X	2
Kendra Kemp																					0
Tom Meadows								X													1
Saba Moslehi																					0
Hannah Nettles											X										1
Julius Ormsby					X	X	X														3
Devon Pike																					0
Melodie Polhemus																					0
Arianna Richardson																					0
Simon Rivera																				X	1

(continued)

FIGURE 2.2 **Sample Classroom Record of Attendance** *(continued)*

October Attendance Record (5th Period) Regular attendance = 0 days, at risk = 1 day, chronic absence = 2–3 days, severe chronic absence = 4+ days

Name	2-Oct	3-Oct	4-Oct	5-Oct	6-Oct	10-Oct	11-Oct	12-Oct	13-Oct	16-Oct	17-Oct	18-Oct	19-Oct	20-Oct	23-Oct	24-Oct	25-Oct	26-Oct	27-Oct	30-Oct	Total Days = 20
Paul Sacks																					0
Lindsey Salfran																					0
Damian Staples								X									X				2
Remi Tanaka																					0
Rhonan Templeton																					0
Amon Vasquez			X																		1
Divina West									X												1
Shadow West																					0
Jessica Zimmerman																					0

Total: 29 students

Number of students with:	0 absences: 15	1 absence (at risk): 9	2–3 absences (chronic): 4	4+ absences (severe chronic): 1

Percentage of students with: 0 absences: 51.7% | 1 absence (at risk): 31% | 2–3 absences (chronic): 13.7% 4+ absences (severe chronic): 3.4%

category. When the first 20-day chart is complete, create another to represent the next 20 days, and continue to use this method throughout the year.

If you notice that a student has reached the chronic absence mark at any point during the chart (e.g., the student has two absences), conduct early interventions, such as a private discussion with the student and a phone call home to remind the student and parents about the importance of attendance. (Early intervention procedures are discussed in Chapter 6.) Using the data shown in Figure 2.2 as an example, you would call Martin Anderson's parents on October 4, after Martin missed two days of school, to check on him and indicate that he is missed when he is absent. Do not wait until the end of the month, when additional absences may have accrued. If you know that a particular student has a history of chronic absence, either in your class or in previous classes, monitor the data for this student more closely so you can provide positive and corrective feedback throughout the month.

Also, periodically examine the data to determine if students miss class more frequently on certain days of the week (e.g., Monday or Friday), or if more absences occur on early-release or late-start days. If you observe these trends across the class, it may be beneficial to implement a motivational system (see Chapter 3) or class lessons (see Chapter 4). If an individual student displays these trends, this can help inform your intervention efforts with that student.

Compile Monthly Classroom Records of Attendance

Plan to keep track of each student's attendance rate for the year by compiling multiple 20-day classroom records or using your data management system to generate each student's cumulative attendance record from the start of the year. If you use a classroom record of attendance (see Figure 2.2), at the end of each 20-day period, transfer the total days of absence for each student to a spreadsheet and add up the number of days students have been absent each month to date (see example in Figure 2.3).

Use the cumulative number of school days to calculate what would be considered regular and at-risk attendance and chronic and severe chronic absence. The following example shows the number of days of absence that would place a student in each category if, at the end of the third month of the school year, there have been 60 days of school:

- Regular attendance: Absent 5 percent or less = 0–3 days absent out of 60 days
- At-risk attendance: Absent between 5.1 percent–9.9 percent = 4–5 days absent out of 60 days

FIGURE 2.3 **Sample Cumulative Classroom Record of Attendance**

Yearly Attendance Record (5th Period) Regular attendance = 5%, at-risk attendance = 5.1%–9.9%, chronic absence = 10%–19.9%, severe chronic absence = 20+%

Absences

Name	Aug. 29–Sept. 30 (20)	Oct. 2–30 (20)	Oct. 31–Dec. 4 (20)	Total Days = 60	Category
Martin Anderson	2	4	3	**9**	Chronic
Selah Artiz	1	0	0	1	
Dante Bjorquist	0	1	1	2	
Joseph Chen	0	0	0	0	
Monique Collins	0	2	1	3	
Jacob Edwards	1	1	2	**4**	At risk
Simone Everett	0	1	3	**4**	At risk
Ivy Farrows	0	0	0	0	
Duncan Hines	2	0	0	2	
Kayaba Iddrisu	0	1	1	2	
Jordan Jones	3	2	3	**8**	Chronic
Kendra Kemp	0	0	0	0	
Tom Meadows	0	1	0	1	
Saba Moslehi	1	0	1	2	
Hannah Nettles	0	1	0	1	
Julius Ormsby	1	3	2	**6**	Chronic
Devon Pike	2	0	1	3	
Melodie Polhemus	1	0	1	2	
Arianna Richardson	0	0	0	0	
Simon Rivera	0	1	0	1	
Paul Sacks	0	0	1	1	
Lindsey Salfran	0	0	0	0	
Damian Staples	1	2	2	**5**	At risk
Remi Tanaka	1	0	1	2	
Rhonan Templeton	0	0	0	0	
Amon Vasquez	0	1	0	1	
Divina West	0	1	3	**4**	At risk
Shadow West	0	0	0	0	
Jessica Zimmerman	1	0	1	2	

Total: 29 students

- Chronic absence: Absent 10 percent–19.9 percent = 6–11 days absent out of 60 days
- Severe chronic absence: Absent 20 percent or more = 12+ days absent out of 60

The teacher using the spreadsheet shown in Figure 2.3 marked those students whose cumulative absences place them in the chronic and at-risk categories at this point in the school year. These data can be used to determine which students require early-stage intervention (see Chapter 6) and to identify students whose absenteeism continues to be a problem despite earlier classroom-based intervention efforts. These students may have a more resistant problem or complex set of concerns that contribute to absenteeism and that may warrant involvement outside the classroom by interventionists or multidisciplinary teams. You can also use the cumulative classroom attendance record to identify students who have made improvements from previous months or who consistently demonstrate regular attendance so that you can provide acknowledgment and rewards as appropriate.

Periodically Analyze Additional Data to Determine Trends and Causes

In the previous sections, we described data that should be collected on an ongoing basis and analyzed approximately once a month (i.e., regular and at-risk attendance and chronic and severe chronic absence). The following data will be analyzed less frequently—a few times a year—to determine causes of absenteeism common to students in your class or school. This data can be collected through a variety of methods, such as filtering your data by time of year or day of week, a student or parent survey, and class discussions. Collected data will help you determine universal efforts that will be beneficial. For example, if the data indicate that many students miss class because they don't wake up on time and miss the bus, you might design lessons and parent tips on setting consistent bedtime and morning routines or how to set an alarm. If the data indicate that many students miss class because of respiratory illnesses like asthma, this may guide you to get an air purifier and request duct inspections in your school, among other targeted efforts. Chapters 3–5 provide additional information on how to tailor your classroom attendance approach based on what you find in the data on trends and causes of absenteeism.

Anonymous Student Survey

Figure 2.4 is an example of an anonymous student survey that can be used to determine common causes of absenteeism. Tailor your survey for the appropriate time of year, age group, and specific factors that may contribute to absenteeism in your community.

Tool 9 in the Grad Nation Community Guidebook (guidebook.americaspromise.org), an online resource for reducing absenteeism and truancy, provides another survey example that examines reasons for tardiness and skipping classes.

Advanced Data Collection

Rather than the simple tally of absences that we described earlier in the chapter, keep a detailed classroom record across each month using codes for different causes of absenteeism to track causes for your class. Codes might include:

- SI: Serious illness: doctor's note or other evidence of serious illness
- MI: Minor or moderate illness; student had cold, headache, or stomachache without other symptoms
- D: Doctor or dentist appointment
- A: Absent for school activity
- X: Unexcused/without parent permission: skipping
- S: Suspension
- T: Tardy
- O: Other (notate the cause on the bottom or back of the record)
- U: Unknown (follow up with the student or parent to determine the cause)

Over time, these detailed classroom attendance records will allow you to see trends in absenteeism across your students, as well as for individuals who have chronic attendance issues.

Anecdotal Teacher Notes

Another way to track common causes of absenteeism is to keep anecdotal notes each day for one month, listing all the causes of absenteeism. When you do not know the specific cause of a student's absence, follow up with

FIGURE 2.4 **Anonymous Student Survey on Causes of Absenteeism**

Approximately how many days have you been absent this year (circle one)?

0–1 2–5 6–9 10–17 18+

Indicate how often the following reasons contributed to your absences.	**Never**	**Once**	**More than once**
I was seriously ill.			
I had a cold, headache, toothache, or other minor or moderate illness.			
I was tired and needed to sleep.			
I had a doctor or dentist appointment.			
I felt anxious or depressed.			
I missed the bus.			
I had no transportation to school.			
It was not safe to walk to school.			
Weather made it too cold or hot to walk.			
I had hygiene reasons (e.g., no clean clothes, no deodorant, felt dirty).			
I had to work.			
I had to take care of younger siblings or other family members.			
I didn't think it would matter if I was absent.			
I didn't think adults at school would notice or care that I was absent.			
I didn't think my peers at school would notice or care that I was absent.			
I didn't think my parents would notice or care that I was absent.			
I did not complete homework or assignments.			
I was not prepared for a test.			
I did not understand the work or expectations in class and didn't want to go.			
My classwork was too hard.			
My classes were boring.			
I was having conflict with peers.			
I was being teased or bullied.			
I was having trouble with a teacher or staff member.			
I was hanging out with friends outside of school.			
I was spending time with my parent or guardian.			
I was using technology (video games, computer, cellphone) I can't use at school.			
I was doing things I wouldn't want to report to the school or my parents.			
I was competing or participating in an outside-of-school sport or activity.			
I was competing or participating in a school-sponsored sport or activity.			

the student or parents to get a better sense of why the student was not in school. At the end of the month, group common causes of absenteeism together to see if any trends emerge.

Class Discussion

Host a class discussion to identify why students miss school. Keep the discussion general, so that no student feels pressured to share a personal situation. Ask general questions like: "When students are absent in this school, what are the most common reasons?" "Without naming names, why do your friends or peers miss school?"

Students might also brainstorm in small groups and list reasons for absences. Then ask each group to rank their reasons in order by how frequently they cause students in the class to be absent.

Reflection Writing Activities

Use a warm-up or exit task to have students reflect on the reasons they are absent or indicate common reasons they see for their peers to be absent. This activity could also be embedded in a longer assignment, such as a class essay, or assignments that require sentence or paragraph writing.

Note

Class discussion and reflection writing activities may also be beneficial when data from other sources (e.g., surveys, coded classroom records, anecdotal teacher notes) point to a trend, but the causes of the trend are not clear or well known. For example, if you discover that students are absent because of difficulties with transportation, but it is not clear what those difficulties are, host a class discussion or have students do a writing reflection to provide more clarity about this cause.

■ ■ ■ ■ ■

Good work in schools starts with good data, and information about attendance is an important tool to guide your classroom improvement efforts. Now that you are collecting and analyzing attendance data on a regular basis, the fun work of strategy implementation begins. In Chapters 3–5, we provide a range of universal classroom strategies that you can use to inform, motivate, and reduce barriers to attendance throughout your class.

Summary of Chapter 2 Tasks

Analyze routines for taking attendance data. Analyze start-of-class routines and methods for taking attendance and recording tardies to determine if attendance is recorded accurately and in a timely manner. Adjust if needed.

Determine how you will monitor classroom attendance across time. Select a method for monitoring each student's attendance and mark in your calendar when you will analyze the data to determine which students fall in the regular and at-risk attendance and chronic and severe chronic absence categories.

Periodically analyze additional data to determine trends and causes. Indicate how you will filter data (e.g., percentage of students in different demographic categories, time-of-year data) and collect additional data (e.g., survey, class discussion, reflection writing activity). Indicate when these data will be analyzed.

3

Speaking the Language of Attendance

For educators to build a classroom culture of attendance, students should hear positive attendance messages and the goal of regular attendance woven throughout their school experience. While this messaging occurs in part through formal lessons on the importance of attendance (as described in Chapter 4), a large part occurs through the more informal strategies described in this chapter. You can think of this work as a campaign to improve the attendance of your whole class. One definition of *campaign* in the Merriam-Webster dictionary is "a connected series of operations designed to bring about a particular result." The work you do to improve attendance in your class can be viewed as an ongoing campaign with connected operations, including initial efforts to build enthusiasm and momentum, and continued efforts across time to sustain students' active engagement in the goal of improving attendance. This is similar to an ad campaign for a new product (e.g., launching and sustaining a new toothpaste brand) or promotion (e.g., Smokey Bear and "Only you can prevent forest fires"). This chapter describes strategies for kicking off your attendance initiative and infusing attendance messages throughout each day with motivational systems and other communications.

Kick Off the Attendance Campaign

Consider how best to launch the attendance campaign with students, families, and, to some extent, relevant community members. Your goal is to generate excitement and interest in the campaign with all relevant stakeholders, especially the students! All kickoff strategies should share the rationale for why attendance is essential for success in school and life and should present information on the critical goal of maintaining regular attendance (missing 5 percent or less) and avoiding chronic absence (absent 10 percent or more). The more times and ways in which you share information about the attendance campaign, the more likely you are to create the momentum needed to change the culture of attendance in your class.

Following are examples of ways to publicize your attendance campaign at the classroom level. If your school is working on creating a schoolwide campaign to address attendance, many procedures may be designed by an attendance team or other entity driving the schoolwide initiative. For example, rather than a title or slogan developed specifically for your classroom, there may be a schoolwide title or slogan that all teachers are expected to use in their attendance communications. As a classroom teacher, your job is to consider how to implement the procedures for the schoolwide campaign with fidelity and enthusiasm and then determine whether additional classroom efforts are needed to enhance attendance improvement efforts with your class(es).

Create a Title or Slogan

Develop a title or slogan for your attendance campaign that speaks to the importance of attendance and the cultural value that you and your class place on being in school and learning every day. This title or slogan should be used like a mantra. Embed it into all subsequent discussions and materials used for your attendance campaign (e.g., posters, graphs of class attendance, communication with families). When possible, incorporate your school mascot, the name of the school, or your class team name. Here are some examples of slogans that might be appropriate for a classroom:

- Mrs. Johnson's Eagles soar to success with regular attendance.
- Students in Class 11 are dependable, persistent, and attend each day.
- Attendance is our classroom key to success!

Hold a Classroom Kickoff

At the outset of your campaign, hold a classroom kickoff meeting specifically focused on teaching students about the importance of attendance and launching the campaign. Provide information on the importance of attendance, but remember to keep the focus on generating enthusiasm. It may also be beneficial to invite parents and guardians to participate in the class event. Consider the following ideas for generating enthusiasm in your class:

- Invite a special guest from the school staff (e.g., the principal, school counselor, or other highly respected staff member) or a local public figure (e.g., sports star, television personality) who can speak to the importance of students being in school every day. Work with the speaker to generate specific talking points related to the attendance campaign.
- Have a group of older students who have good grades and regular attendance speak to the students about how their success is dependent on being in school each day. For example, invite a group of selected 5th graders to speak to a primary or lower-intermediate class. Or invite a group of 11th- or 12th-grade high school students to speak to middle school students or incoming freshmen. Work with the student speakers to generate specific talking points or a presentation related to the attendance campaign.
- Create an attendance chant, or use your class's selected attendance slogan and have different groups of students compete to give the most convincing cheer.
- Introduce class motivational systems and possible rewards that will be used in the subsequent term or semester. (See pp. 55–62 for examples of classroom motivational systems and rewards.)
- Conduct one or more fun activities related to the attendance initiative. For example:
  - Have students create posters advertising the attendance initiative and hang the posters throughout the classroom and in the hallway near the class.
  - Have students participate in a team-building activity that demonstrates the importance of all students being present and working together.

– Use puffy paint or permanent markers to create t-shirts with the attendance slogan. Or get your class slogan screen printed on shirts and do a tie-dyeing activity with the class.

Send an Initial Letter Home

Send home an initial letter and pass out the letter at back-to-school night or other parent presentations. The letter should inform parents about the attendance initiative, indicate why it is important for students to regularly attend school, and provide information about measures you and the school will take to partner with families to problem-solve when it is difficult to get a student to school regularly. The tone of this initial letter should be welcoming and supportive. Avoid placing too much emphasis on punitive measures, such as fines or truancy court. See Figure 3.1 for an example. Note that the letter refers to an attendance chart, which is described in the next paragraph.

Provide an Attendance Chart

Send home a chart that the student and family can use to monitor absences across the year. Inform the students, and families, that any time they are absent, they should fill in one of the spaces on the chart. Design the chart to reflect the number of absences that would place the student in the regular attendance category at the end of the year—for example, if your school year is 180 days, include nine spaces for absences (180 x 5 percent = 9). If possible, color-code the absences: Absences one to nine should be green, and absences 10 and up should change to yellow or red to indicate increasing risk. (*Note*: Adapt these numbers to reflect the number of days of school on your school calendar. If your school has 160 days of school, for example, 5 percent would be eight days, so the chart should have eight green spaces.)

Be sure to note that a student is at increased risk for academic difficulties and other struggles at school with each subsequent absence beyond the spaces provided on the chart. Print the chart on card stock or laminate it.

The goal of this chart is to provide a tool for busy students and families to maintain a better sense of how many absences the student has accumulated in the course of the year. See Figure 3.2 for a sample attendance chart.

FIGURE 3.1 **Initial Attendance Letter**

DEDICATED TO ACADEMIC EXCELLENCE

Loganville Middle School
4321 Any Street
Townsville, State 54321

Dear Families,

I am looking forward to a great year, with students in classes and ready to learn every day!

I have learned that students who miss even a few days of school each month are at far greater risk of academic failure and dropout than students who attend regularly. In my classroom, we have set the goal that every student attends regularly (has nine or fewer absences in a year). We will be using numerous motivational systems and other strategies to encourage students to attend every day possible!

Because attendance is so important, please send your student to school every day unless he or she has a contagious illness or is running a fever. I have included a chart with this letter that can help you keep track of your student's absences. Whenever your student misses class, fill in one of the spaces, and try to stay as far under the goal of nine or fewer absences as possible.

If your child is at risk of missing too much school, please feel free to contact me at 555-1234 to discuss ways that we can work together to solve any barriers to attendance or other concerns. I will be monitoring each student's attendance across the year so we can quickly identify and provide support when the number of absences puts a student at risk. I am happy to work with you to help your student attend regularly and have greater opportunities for success.

Sincerely,

Mrs. Rodriguez
6th Grade Math and Science Teacher

Source: From *Foundations: A Proactive and Positive Behavior Support System* (3rd Ed., Modules A–F), by R. Sprick, S. Isaacs, M. Booher, J. Sprick, and P. Rich, 2014, Eugene, Oregon: Ancora Publishing. Copyright 2014 by Ancora Publishing. Adapted with permission.

FIGURE 3.2 **Generic Attendance Chart**

Date	Date	Date	Date	Date	Date	Date	Date	Date	Absence 10+
Absence 1 Reason:	Absence 2 Reason:	Absence 3 Reason:	Absence 4 Reason:	Absence 5 Reason:	Absence 6 Reason:	Absence 7 Reason:	Absence 8 Reason:	Absence 9 Reason:	Your student is at increasing risk for academic difficulties and school failure with each absence beyond this point.

Source: From *Foundations: A Proactive and Positive Behavior Support System* (3rd Ed., Modules A–F), by R. Sprick, S. Isaacs, M. Booher, J. Sprick, and P. Rich, 2014, Eugene, Oregon: Ancora Publishing. Copyright 2014 by Ancora Publishing.

Informally Emphasize Attendance

One of the best ways to create a culture of attendance is for teachers and other staff to emphasize the importance of attendance in many subtle and frequent ways. These range from greeting students by name each day to welcoming students back after absences to setting up informal procedures to contact students who have been absent. Find multiple ways to connect with students and emphasize the importance of being in school regularly. It may be useful to put some regular reminders in your calendar to consider ways to informally infuse an attendance message into interactions with students.

Note

The following strategies are meaningful for all students, but they are especially important for students who are at risk or have histories of chronic absenteeism, disengagement, or behavioral or academic struggles in school.

Greet Students and Welcome Them After an Absence

It is easy to underestimate the power of a simple greeting and saying to a student, "I missed you," or, "Our class missed you yesterday." However, when staff welcome students by name each day and follow up when a student has been absent, this can go a long way toward making a student feel noticed and appreciated. It also provides a subtle accountability mechanism, as students will have to respond (hopefully to a teacher they respect and admire) about the reasons for the absence. Simple messages, like "I'm glad to have you back in class," or, "Is everything OK? I noticed you've been gone the last few days," can be very powerful in helping achieve these goals.

Plan to greet students by name at the door as they enter your room. Some teachers add a personal handshake or other greeting that can increase the likelihood that the interaction is meaningful for the student. It may also be beneficial to review the previous day's attendance record prior to class so that you can make a point of providing a little extra attention when greeting absent students when they return. This is especially important in secondary school, when you have many different groups of students.

Jessica remembers the following story from her own school experience when she considers the importance of greeting students and welcoming them back after an absence. "When I was in elementary school, everyone's favorite staff member was the cafeteria and recess supervisor. Whenever someone came back from an absence, she always came up to that student in the lunch line to say, 'You were absent yesterday, and I missed you!' Not only did she know who was absent, but she also authentically made all students feel like she cared if they were gone and looked forward to seeing them when they came back to school."

Jessica found out later that before lunch each day, this staff member would look at the previous day's attendance and identify students who were absent so that she could make a point of greeting them when they returned. This simple act made all the students feel noticed and valued.

Call Students When They Have Been Absent for More Than a Day

When a student has been absent for two or more days in a row or spread out across a one-month period, it is extremely valuable to call and say something like, "We miss you when you are gone and look forward to having you back in class soon." These calls do not need to be lengthy or involved but should send a simple message that the student is noticed and missed when absent. This is especially important in middle and high school, when students may feel that no one notices or cares when they are absent. In fact, 32 percent of students who skipped school reported that adults in the school (teachers, administrators, and attendance officers) rarely or never notice that they are gone, and an additional 32 percent said that adults in school only sometimes notice (Get Schooled Foundation, 2012). All students should feel that someone notices and authentically cares whenever they are not in school.

Jessica recalls that when she was in high school, she knew the school's attendance policy. It stated that after seven *unexcused* absences in a semester, a student's grade would be reduced by one letter grade for each subsequent absence. This did not include excused absences. Jessica was a martial artist and sometimes skipped classes to train and work out. She kept track of her unexcused absences, marking a tally in the corner of the divider in her binder for each class period. She made sure to never go above the seven absences for any given class, and her attendance never triggered any sort of intervention or concern by the school. Considering that she had excused absences as well, she is sure that her attendance record would have shown that she was chronically absent for most of high school. Luckily, she was able to compensate academically; however, Jessica wonders how much more she would have learned if she hadn't missed so much school!

The point of this story is that no teacher, administrator, or other school staff member ever asked Jessica where she had been the previous day, much less said they would call her parents or initiate other intervention efforts if these problematic attendance patterns continued. She had high respect for her teachers, and if any one of them had asked her where she had been, she would never have skipped that class again. Jessica would not have wanted to lie or tell them she skipped the class. The truth was that she thought it didn't matter if she missed some school, and no one ever told her otherwise.

When a student exhibits a pattern of problematic absenteeism, more in-depth discussions and phone calls may be warranted. See Chapter 6 for early-stage classroom interventions, such as phone calls home and planned discussions, that can be implemented to address ongoing patterns of absenteeism.

Encourage Students to Call One Another When a Student Has Been Absent

In some classrooms, teachers institute a buddy or small-group system in which each student is connected with one to three other students. When students are absent, their partner or team can call to tell them they are missed and encourage them to come back as soon as possible. Provide possible talking points for students so that they know how to relay encouragement in positive ways (e.g., "I hope you get better soon!" "We will be thinking about you until you come back!").

Use Classroom Motivational Systems

Once your attendance campaign is launched, the work of maintaining momentum across time begins. Consider how to keep an ongoing focus on attendance and try to make the initiative compelling and fun. Classroom motivational systems are simple and efficient ways to place ongoing emphasis on the attendance initiative, and you can be highly creative in making them engaging and exciting for students. Classroom motivational systems have numerous benefits:

- Daily tracking and discussion of attendance in a motivational system sends a regular message that attendance is important.
- Awareness of attendance trends is heightened for the students, parents, and the teacher through the routine of the system.
- Students take pride in how their attendance contributes to class progress in the system.
- Group motivational systems encourage students to work together and can be beneficial for creating a sense of community and collective goals.
- They are minimally invasive on class time and teacher preparation time.
- For some students, the rewards earned or slightly competitive aspects of a system may be highly motivating.
- They can be easily adapted to maintain interest and provide a needed boost during times when absenteeism is most problematic.

One teacher shared with us that she was skeptical that a simple motivational system would work for her students. She taught in a school with very low attendance rates, and she said, "I have to admit, I was really doubtful that a small thing like a mystery prize in an envelope with no monetary value would have any weight for the kids at all. Ever since we started this reward system, we have had way more kids present for eight days straight! Every time a kid comes in and puts a group at its goal for number of students present, they all get really excited, so the kid feels awesome for coming to school. Thank you so much for this!"

It may be beneficial to select one or more systems (e.g., classroom attendance chart) to carry out throughout the entire year and bring in other systems (e.g., raffle, 100 squares, competition between teams in the class) during particularly problematic times of year or when enthusiasm for the attendance initiative is waning.

The following section provides general principles for creating and implementing motivational systems and gives examples of classroom motivational systems for students. See Appendix A for examples of classroom and individual student reinforcers that can be selected for any of these systems.

General Principles for Reinforcement Systems

Whatever reinforcement system or systems you choose to use, the following principles for designing and delivering the reinforcement system will increase the likelihood that the system motivates students and helps you reach desired classroom goals. These suggestions will help you avoid some of the pitfalls that can make reinforcement systems less effective or even detrimental. This section is followed by step-by-step explanations of a variety of different classroom-based systems.

Secondary school teachers or teachers who see many different classes of students in elementary school may want to vary the systems used for different class periods throughout the day. Your highly responsible, highly self-motivated group in first period may warrant different procedures for the motivational system (or even an entirely different system) than your sixth-period remedial class that has numerous students with behavioral, academic, and motivational challenges. Use the following suggestions to modify your systems for different groups.

Set a Reasonable Yet Challenging Goal

If the system requires students to meet a specific goal to progress in the system, set a goal that pushes them to do more than they are currently doing without being so far out of reach that there is no hope for success. For example, in a whole-class daily attendance system, students earn a point each day the class attendance meets a certain predetermined goal. While you may be tempted to set a goal of perfect attendance, do this only when the whole-class attendance is already fairly good (e.g., your first-period group currently averages 28 or 29 students a day, so set a goal of 30 out of 30 students). If average daily attendance for the class is lower, set a short-term goal that is only slightly higher than the current attendance (e.g., in your sixth-period group, only 24 out of 30 students attend class on average, so set a goal of 26 out of 30 students). Once students are consistently meeting the short-term goal and have earned one or more rewards at that level, you can move the goal up an incremental amount (e.g., once students are meeting the goal of 26 out of 30 students consistently, move the goal line to 28 out of 30).

Allow Students to Earn Rewards Quickly at First

If your system involves rewards for students, ensure that students have a high probability of earning initial rewards in a relatively short time span. For example, if students earn a point for each day that they meet their whole-class attendance goal, allow them to receive their first reward when they accumulate three points (i.e., they meet the goal on three separate days). As student attendance improves, you can gradually lengthen the time intervals for earning the reward. For example, allow students to earn a reward when they have earned five points, then eight points, then 10 points. At the school where Tricia worked, classes advanced within their motivational system by filling in a letter on a word for each day they met their goal. As the class filled in a word, they received a certificate and were acknowledged on the morning announcements. These words became progressively longer with each success (e.g., wow, cool, super).

If you reach a point where students are consistently posting high attendance rates without needing rewards very often, have a whole-class discussion to determine if students are ready to abandon the reward-based system. If students agree that they can maintain their positive behavior without the system, set a classwide goal (e.g., The students in Mrs. Johnson's fourth-period class agree to continue attending regularly each day they are not seriously ill without needing a reward system). Continue providing positive feedback and occasionally a small, unexpected reward when students continue to meet your expectations. Alternatively, fade the reward-based system by introducing invisible ink rewards as described on p. 58 and gradually increasing the length of time between rewards.

Avoid Arbitrary Time Limits

Have students work toward goals that are not consecutive or time sensitive. For example, a teacher might set up a whole-class system as described in previous paragraphs, where students earn points for meeting a daily whole-class attendance goal. However, if the teacher says, "You will earn your reward when the class meets the goal on three *consecutive* days," this can create numerous problems. With consecutive goals—those that require students to meet the goal a certain number of times in a row—students may become frustrated and give up on the system if they come close to meeting the goal several times and then lose it when they don't meet their goal for a day. Also avoid systems with arbitrary time limits—"You will earn your reward when the class meets the goal at least three days *this week.*" A system that sets a date by which the students must earn the reward or else start over is risky because if students have difficulty at the beginning of the system, they may realize there is no way to make up lost ground, and so they give up trying. For example, in the system where students can earn a reward by meeting the goal three out of five days in a week, if the students do not meet the goal on any of the first three days of the week, they may realize that there is no way they can get three points by Friday. They therefore have no incentive to improve attendance on Thursday and Friday. Or, if students met their goal by Wednesday, they have no incentive to push for great class attendance on Thursday and Friday.

Instead of consecutive goals or those with arbitrary time limits, allow students to earn rewards whenever they accumulate the desired number of points or other criterion for earning rewards. For example, the class will earn a reward whenever it has three days meeting of the goal for class attendance, whether that is three days in a row or three days spread out across a series of weeks. This will help you emphasize to students that it is up to them how quickly or how long it takes for them to earn desired rewards.

Seek Student Input on Possible Rewards

Work with students to determine a range of rewards to be used within selected reinforcement systems. Your systems will be far more powerful if students know they might earn one or more items or activities that they are personally interested in. Rewards should range from small, no-cost or low-cost rewards, like a templated positive letter sent home to each student or a class cheer, to higher-value rewards. Higher-value rewards cost more money or time to provide (e.g., a special treat delivered to students, or a movie or game during class time). Appendix A provides a list of possible individual and whole-class rewards. To gain student input, consider copying this list for each of your students and asking them to indicate which ones they would be interested in earning. You could also spend a few minutes of class time brainstorming possible rewards with students. Tell them that anything goes for brainstorming as long as it is not immoral, illegal, or outside school and district policies! While you will have final say over the items and activities that are included in the reward system, you would like their input about what they would be interested in earning.

It is always fun to hear from schools about the rewards that are highly motivating to their students. We are often surprised at how eager students are to earn simple and inexpensive rewards. For one elementary group at

McLean Elementary School in Wichita, Kansas, a desired reward was "Crazy Sock Day," when all the students wore crazy socks to school. The teacher had the students lie down in a circle with their feet in the center so he could take a picture of their crazy socks. An elementary teacher at a different school found that her students most wanted to earn a "flashlight reading party," where the teacher turned off all the lights and students read silently with flashlights for 15 minutes. At an alternative high school, the reward that students most wanted to earn was "Potluck Day," when students brought food from home to share with their classmates.

Use Elements of Mystery to Generate Excitement

It is next to impossible to find a reward that every student in the class will be excited to earn. Reinforcement systems can also become incredibly expensive with money and time if you try to select rewards that are highly motivating for all students. The way to avoid these pitfalls is to include an element of mystery in the system by using Mystery Motivators or a spinner. Rather than telling students, "If you complete this behavior, you will earn this specific reward," let students know that if they meet the criterion set within the reinforcement system, they will earn one randomly selected reward from a set of preselected rewards.

With a Mystery Motivator system, select a certain number of possible rewards, including many low-cost or no-cost rewards, a few medium-cost rewards, and one or two high-cost, high-value rewards. Write each reward on a slip of paper and place it in a bag or box labeled with a question mark or "Mystery Motivator." When students earn their reward, draw one of the slips from the bag and reveal what students have earned. The beauty of this is that it allows you to include a variety of rewards that are highly motivating to students while also limiting the cost, as students are more likely to earn one of the lower-cost items than the one or two high-cost, high-value items.

With a spinner system, create a game spinner with five to 10 numbered sections of varying sizes. Each numbered section is paired with a possible reward (e.g., 1 = five minutes early to lunch, 2 = hat day, 3 = snowball fight with recycled paper for two minutes). High-cost rewards should be assigned to the smallest slices on the spinner so that students have a small chance to earn them, but a greater chance of earning the low- and medium-cost items or activities. A student spins the spinner, and the class receives that reward when they meet their classwide goal. Free online spinners are also available—search for "online game spinner."

These systems provide an additional way to increase motivation at the outset of the system by using more high-value rewards, which fade across time as students demonstrate success. When you start the system, consider using a greater number of slips with high-value rewards in relation to the number of possible lower-value rewards (e.g., include three low-cost, three medium-cost, and four high-cost reward slips) so that students have a greater chance to earn something of higher value. Or assign one or more of the high-cost, high-value rewards to a large slice on the spinner. Once students demonstrate success, begin gradually adjusting the system to make it more challenging. For example, change the slips to include four low-cost, four medium-cost, and two high-cost rewards, or reassign slices of the spinner so that high-cost items are on the smallest spaces.

Preplan for Any Likely Contingencies

Think through possible pitfalls or ways that students may get frustrated by the system, and then work to correct for these possibilities in advance. One likely possibility is that students may become frustrated when they earn a large reward and do not receive it right away. Correct for this by teaching students that some rewards require more time and effort to plan. Tell students that if they earn such a reward, it does not mean they will get it on that day, but that you will start actively planning when the reward will be delivered. For example, one of the largest rewards in Jessica's classroom was a field trip. But students knew that if they earned that reward, it meant that she would start planning and making arrangements (e.g., transportation, chaperones, parent permissions) with a goal of having the field trip within two or three months.

Another possible pitfall is that one student may consistently fail to meet the expectations or actively sabotage the system, making it so the rest of the class does not progress toward rewards. If you notice this occurring or anticipate that this will be a problem, there are a few possible safeguards. The first is to design the system so that students can meet the goal regardless of the individual student's behavior. Then allow the class to earn additional points or rewards if the individual student also meets the criterion. For example, if one student consistently struggles with attendance, you could make the goal for class attendance 29 out of 30 students, but if 30 out of 30 students attend, the class earns two points instead of one. Another possibility is to take these students out of the calculation for the whole-group reward (e.g., the goal for class attendance is 29 out of 29 students) and put them on an individual reinforcement system (see Chapter 6 for individual student interventions and motivational systems).

Explicitly Teach Students the Expectations for the System

Prepare one or more lessons to teach students all aspects of how the system works. Ensure that you clarify expectations for student behavior and how students demonstrate progress toward their goals. You will need to clarify details, such as whether a tardy student can be counted as present and whether a tardy will be considered an absence after a certain time (e.g., a student who is more than 10 minutes late will not be counted as present in the reinforcement system). After you teach how the system will work, verify students' understanding by asking questions. Also, consider asking for feedback on ways to strengthen the system to increase students' motivation to participate.

Maintain Enthusiasm for the System and for the Benefits to the Class

Your energy and enthusiasm are critical factors in the success or failure of the system. Even the most well-designed motivational systems are likely to fail when teachers project an attitude that this is something they *have* to do rather than something they are invested in doing and excited about because it will increase student success. It is also important to keep your focus and energy on the benefits that come from increased attendance rather than on the rewards themselves. While you can periodically pump up students by ruminating on possible rewards (e.g., "Only two more days of meeting our goal before we can open the mystery envelope and see what you've earned!"), it is far more beneficial to keep your feedback focused on what students are doing and the benefits this brings to their success and the class (e.g., "We've had five days of meeting our goal. I'm so impressed with how much progress we are making when we have everyone in class working together!").

Periodically Revise the Rewards or the System

Over time, any system is likely to get stale without modifications. Consider ways to reinvigorate interest in the system by changing up possible rewards, making it more challenging for students to earn desired rewards, or switching to a different system.

Whole-Class Reinforcement Systems

The following are examples of whole-class systems that can be implemented in the first period or hour of the day, each class throughout the day, or in a daily advisory or homeroom class.

Daily Classroom Attendance Graph

Create a large poster with a line graph or bar chart displaying the number of students in class in attendance each day (see Figure 3.3 for a sample graph). For secondary teachers or elementary teachers who see multiple groups of students throughout the day, create a poster for each class period and assemble it into a flip chart (e.g., use binder rings to clip the posters together). Draw a goal line on the chart that is specific to the class, based on current attendance rates, and that is within reach but pushes the class to do better than they've done in the past. As students are successful in meeting this goal, gradually move the goal line up. Enhance the system by using Mystery Motivators or a spinner reward when students meet their goal for a certain number of days (see p. 52 for how to use a Mystery Motivator or spinner system).

Display the poster at the front of the classroom or in another highly visible location. At the beginning of each day (or period in secondary school), count the number of students in the room and add it to the graph. During this ritual, continue to emphasize the importance of attendance for student success and the classroom culture. Provide positive feedback for students who are present and work to problem solve with students when they have difficulties meeting the goal.

One elementary teacher we worked with made a modification to the Daily Classroom Attendance Graph concept by making paper chains reflecting student attendance. Each day when her 1st grade students entered the classroom, she had them grab strips of colored construction paper and write their names on them using their best handwriting. As they conducted their morning attendance routine and students worked on quiet independent activities the teacher walked around and personally greeted students and thanked them for being in class. She also looped the student's strip into a circle and stapled it to a class chain with all the links from students in attendance that day. At the end of this ritual, she hung the strip from the ceiling along one wall and counted the number of links to see if the class met its goal for the day. The wall with chains from each day became a powerful symbol of the class working together and a reminder of the importance of every student attending to

FIGURE 3.3 **Graph of Daily Classroom Attendance**

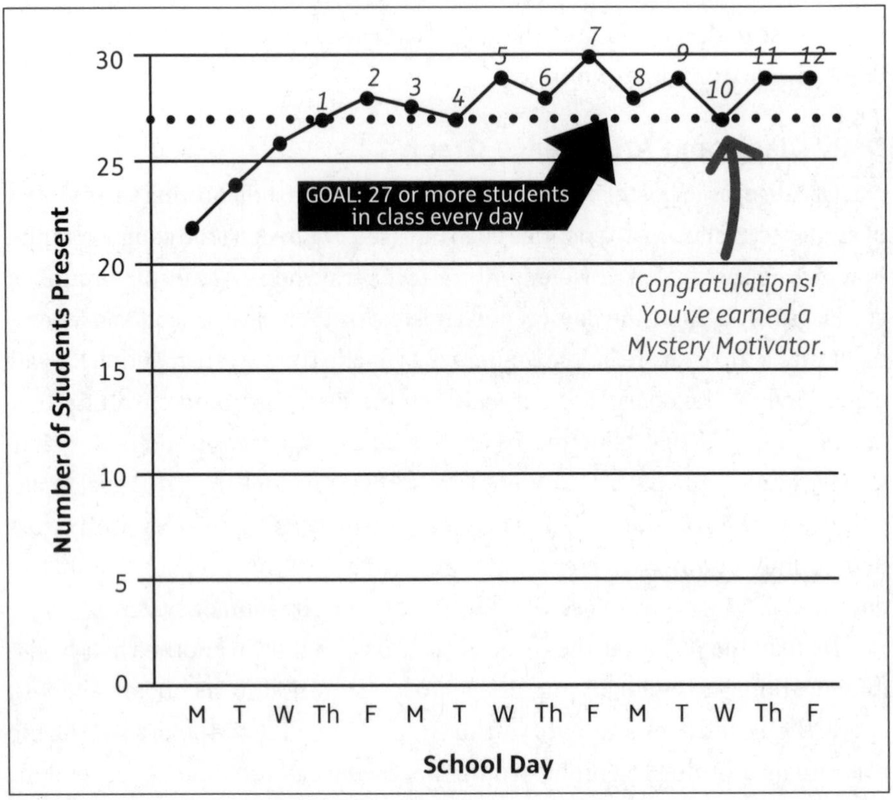

make a link in the chain. This ritual also provided an opportunity for the teacher to personally connect with and welcome each student at the beginning of class.

A high school teacher used the Daily Classroom Attendance Graph but used a bar chart instead of a line graph. She designed a chart for each period throughout the day and clipped them together using binder rings. She placed the graphs next to the door and had each student fill in one unit on the bar for the day as they entered her class. Before each class, she greeted students as they entered the room and filled in the chart.

Classroom Group Contingency

This system can be used with a whole class or a small group of students, and it would also be appropriate for addressing tardies (e.g., track the number of days that students are in class on time and ready to learn).

Write the following numbers on individual slips of paper or note cards (one number on each card): 1, 2, 3, 3, 4, 4, 4, 5, 5, 5. There will be 10 pieces of paper or note cards when you are finished. Put them in a paper bag or other container that students cannot see through.

Each morning, track attendance and praise all students for attending. You may wish to keep track on a weekly log or have students mark their own logs, filling in a box for each day they are present (see Figures 3.4 and 3.5). If you use the teacher log, this should be a discreet record for you, not a publicly posted display, to ensure that no student is publicly shamed for poor attendance during a particular week or across time.

FIGURE 3.4 **Teacher Log of Weekly Attendance**

Week of:

	Mon	Tues	Wed	Thurs	Fri	Total for Week
Monique Alverez	X	X			X	3
Susie Anderson	X	X	X	X	X	5
Dustin Barnett	X	X	X	X	X	5
Jorie Baymont	X		X	X	X	4
Valerie Bijorquist	X	X	X	X	X	5
Dominique Chambers	X	X	X	X	X	5
Simon Covington					X	1
Sekou Camara	X	X	X	X	X	5
Destiny Favrou	X	X	X		X	4

FIGURE 3.5 **Student Log of Weekly Attendance**

Weekly Attendance Log

Name:

	Mon	Tues	Wed	Thurs	Fri	Total for Week
Week 1	X	X		X	X	4
Week 2	X	X	X	X	X	5
Week 3						
Week 4						
Week 5						

On Friday morning, have one student randomly select one of the numbered slips of paper from the bag or container. All students in the class whose attendance for the week matched or exceeded the number drawn from the bag will receive the Mystery Motivator or spinner class reward (see p. 52 for how to use a Mystery Motivator or spinner system). Those who attended fewer days than the number drawn do not receive the reward.

Over time, you can make it more difficult for students to earn rewards by removing one of the lower-numbered note cards (e.g., a two or three) and replacing it with a higher-numbered note card (e.g., four or five). Gradually removing the lower numbers makes it less likely that students will earn the reward if they miss days during the week. However, always keep the note card with the number 1—even when a student misses four days at the beginning of the week, there is an incentive to attend on Friday. At an advanced stage of the system, the note cards will read: 1, 3, 5, 5, 5, 5, 5, 5, 5, 5.

(Monthly) Class Group Contingency Adaptation: Consider whether to adapt the preceding procedure so that the Mystery Motivator is drawn once a month rather than once a week. The greater the attendance problems across a whole class, the more frequently rewards should be delivered; however, if attendance is generally fairly good or a weekly drawing is overwhelming, you might conduct the reward procedures monthly. For a 20-day month, adapt the numbers on the note cards to something like: 10, 16, 18, 18, 19, 19, 19, 20, 20, 20. Remember to keep one number card relatively low so that even if students have highly problematic attendance during the first half or three-quarters of the month, there is still a small chance they will earn the reward if they attend for the remainder of the month.

Invisible Ink Attendance Rewards

Use a special invisible ink marker or decoding pen to mark a certain number of invisible *x*'s on a calendar. (*Note:* These pens are available at many office supply stores and can also be found online by searching "decoding pens," "invisible ink pens," or "secret message pens.") Ensure that the *x*'s are placed at random intervals so that some are close together and some are far apart. This ensures that students do not begin to expect an *x* on any predictable schedule. At the start of the system, include more *x*'s within the first month so that students earn rewards more frequently at first, and then fade the number of *x*'s placed on the calendar as students demonstrate success with the system.

Each day, have a student use the pen to reveal whether an x is marked on that day of the calendar. If an *x* is revealed, select from the Mystery Motivators or use a spinner to determine the reward earned by all students in attendance that day. Any student who is absent for the day does not earn the reward. (*Note:* With this system, it may be appropriate to use relatively small rewards so that a student who is absent on a day when a reward is earned does not feel unduly penalized for one day of absence. For example, include things like two minutes of time chatting with friends or five minutes of silly YouTube videos rather than a reward that requires a whole period or more.)

If it is difficult to obtain invisible-ink or decoder pens, you can achieve a similar result using adhesive dots and sticky notes. Place adhesive dots at random intervals on the calendar. Then cover up each school day with a sticky note so that students can't see which days have the dots and which days are blank. Each day, remove the sticky note to reveal whether it is a reward day or not. One caution with this system: Make sure you place the calendar in a location where students cannot sneak a peek at where the dots are placed. You don't want to be constantly policing students, who will naturally want to take a look!

Classroom Raffle

Randomly select several days each month and distribute raffle tickets to every student in attendance on that day. The raffle system can be combined with the invisible ink concept described previously, as you use an invisible ink marker to mark random days on the calendar and each morning color over the day square on the calendar to reveal if it is a raffle ticket distribution day. At the end of the month, gather all raffle tickets for entry into a classroom drawing. Provide a range of prizes for individual students, including many small prizes, a moderate number of medium prizes, and a few grand prizes. During problematic times of year (e.g., the week before and after a major break), increase the frequency of raffle ticket distribution and prize delivery so that students in attendance during these times have a greater chance of winning the prizes.

Attendance Squares (Sprick, 2009)

This system is a combination of tic-tac-toe and bingo. Create a square (a 4 × 4 grid) and number the spaces from 1 to 16. Place the chart in a prominent place in the room. Get two containers (bowls or hats, for example) and 16 small tokens, such as poker chips, small tagboard squares, or popsicle sticks. On each token, write a number from 1 to 16. Place all of them into one of the two containers.

Set a goal for class attendance that is specific to the class, based on current attendance rates. Remember that the goal should be within reach, but push the class to do better than they've done in the past. For example, if the class averaged 29 out of 35 students in the last week, set a goal of 32 out of 35 students to start. As students are successful in meeting this goal, gradually make the goal more difficult. Each day that the class meets the goal, have a student draw one of the tokens from the full container. Identify the number written on the token, then fill in—initial or color—the space on the chart with the same number. Place the token into the empty (second) container. When four squares in a row—horizontally, vertically, or diagonally—have been filled in, the entire class gets one of the group rewards selected from the Mystery Motivator container or spinner (see p. 52 for how to use a Mystery Motivator or spinner system). Once a full row has been completed and a reward given, erase the filled-in square, and return all the drawn tokens to the original container. Begin the system again. To make the system more difficult across time, begin using larger grids (e.g., 6 × 6, 8 × 8, 10 × 10) and add tokens to match the number of squares on the larger grid (e.g., 6 × 6 grid = 36 tokens, 8 × 8 grid = 64 tokens, 10 × 10 grid = 100 tokens).

Classroom Attendance Awards

Hold a monthly or term/semester celebration of attendance. Use this opportunity to reteach and show enthusiasm for the class's collective efforts to build a culture of attendance.

We recommend focusing on awards that recognize students in the regular attendance category and those with significantly improved attendance. In many schools, perfect attendance is celebrated and rewarded, but these awards are problematic because they may encourage some students to come to school when they have a contagious illness and should stay home. They are also not attainable or equitable for some students whose absences are related to chronic illness or situations that are out of their control (e.g., parents who can't or won't get students to school regularly). If you wish to include recognition for perfect attendance, we recommend that these awards be limited to perfect attendance within a month rather than a term or full year. In this way, you can remind students that if they need to stay home because they are seriously ill, they can try for the perfect attendance award the next month.

Friendly Class Competitions

Create friendly competitions within a class among teams of students, across classes in partnership with other teachers, or across periods in a secondary school. With any friendly competition, teach corresponding lessons about necessary social and interactional skills that will make the system successful. For example, teach a brief lesson to students about how to encourage peers to attend, as opposed to bullying or threatening them. You might also teach skills, like how to be good winners and good losers, and ways that students can work together toward improvements in attendance (e.g., arranging carpools, providing morning calls or check-ins for encouragement). Friendly competitions might include:

- The small group or class with the most improved average attendance rate over the previous month (see Chapter 2 for how to calculate the average attendance rate for a class)
- The small group or class with the highest average attendance rate each month or week

---

From the Field: Attendopoly

Heather Graves and Jessica Morris were 5th grade teachers in Wichita, Kansas. They identified improving attendance as a critical priority for their students, so they got creative in developing a friendly class competition. Students were placed in teams of four, with students having the best and worst attendance evenly distributed across the groups. The teachers created a Monopoly-type game board on their SMARTboard, and they used individual student names as the property names on the board.

Each morning, the class played one round of Attendopoly. In order for a team to roll and progress in the game, each teammate in the group had to be present. If anyone on a team was absent, the team would not roll but could still collect rent for the day. If the team had anyone absent (even a different team member) two days in a row, the team was sent to the "jail" space and could not collect rent or pass Go!

This system was a phenomenal success. The teachers reported numerous benefits, including:

- Students learned to rely on one another.
- Students called other students when they were absent or tardy to check on them and encourage them to come to school.
- Students celebrated when teammates arrived, which helped create a strong and supportive community.
- Students learned how to work together and play games.

- This system facilitated great conversations with the group, like how to schedule medical appointments outside school hours.
- It allowed the teachers to have productive, problem-solving conversations with tough parents.

The teachers reported that the five-minute time commitment each day was worth it, as it created a fun start to the day and significantly improved the class's attendance. In the months prior to the system, this class had the worst attendance of any in the school. After beginning the system, the class earned "most improved" and won the school's attendance award for best class attendance every month for the rest of the year.

■ ■ ■ ■ ■

The strategies in this chapter are some of the most powerful for building enthusiasm and momentum for your attendance efforts. We cannot underestimate the importance of a fun and welcoming atmosphere for students, which can be built in part through the motivational and other strategies described in this chapter. When used in conjunction with the strategies in Chapter 4, "If You Want It, Teach It! Delivering Attendance Lessons," we solidify students' understanding of why attendance is critical to their success and help ensure that they want to be in school each day.

Summary of Chapter 3 Tasks

Conduct activities to kick off the attendance campaign. Create a title or slogan for your attendance campaign, and design other kickoff activities.

Informally emphasize attendance with all students. Place reminders in your calendar (e.g., once a month) to consider ways to reinvigorate your attendance efforts and prompt yourself to informally emphasize the importance of attendance. Determine a range of strategies for providing this emphasis, such as:

- Greeting students by name
- Welcoming students back after absence
- Calling students when they have been absent more than a day

- Setting up procedures for students to call one another when a peer is absent

Use classroom motivational systems. Select one or more classroom motivational systems. Work through the following general principles to ensure the system is effectively designed and implemented:

- Set a reasonable yet challenging goal.
- Allow students to earn rewards quickly at first, then less frequently as they demonstrate success.
- Avoid arbitrary time limits.
- Seek student input on possible rewards.
- Use elements of mystery to generate excitement and allow the possibility for higher-value rewards.
- Preplan for any likely contingencies.
- Explicitly teach students the expectations for the system and how they will earn rewards.
- Maintain enthusiasm for the system and for the benefits to the class in the form of improved attendance and teamwork.
- Periodically revise the rewards or the system.

4

If You Want It, Teach It! Delivering Attendance Lessons

Why should we teach students about the importance of attendance? It's easy, it's cheap, and it may significantly reduce the problem of absenteeism! Many students simply do not understand that attendance is a critical factor that can influence their success or failure, not only in your classroom, but in life. In a survey of students in grades 8–12 who reported skipping school a few times a month or more, only 18 percent believed it was "very likely" that they would personally fall behind in their classes if they skipped once a week (Get Schooled Foundation, 2012). Many students do not understand that missing only two days a month could set them on a path toward dropping out of school. Attendance lessons should be designed to help your students understand that attendance is a critical variable for passing classes and graduating. These lessons should also emphasize that students are more likely to be successful with future goals when they exhibit habits of dependability and reliability as shown when they are in class every day, on time, and ready to learn. Students may also require explicit lessons on topics that contribute to attendance (e.g., appropriate sleep habits, how to stay healthy during cold and flu season, coping with/problem solving bullying situations). In this chapter, you will learn how to develop effective lessons to build a classroom culture of attendance. This chapter also provides numerous sample lessons, examples of possible topics for lessons, and examples of how attendance lessons can be incorporated into grade-level standards.

Teach Formal Lessons About Attendance

All students should receive lessons that emphasize the importance of attendance and teach them how to set and meet the goal of regular attendance (e.g., "I will be present at least 171 out of 180 days this year"). These lessons should also emphasize the importance of being on time. Depending on the magnitude of attendance problems in your classroom, these lessons may occur as infrequently as a few times a year to as frequently as a weekly or daily lesson. Lessons that focus specifically on attendance should be relatively short (i.e., 5–15 minutes) and age appropriate and help students understand that their success depends on being in school regularly. You can also seek out opportunities to incorporate concepts related to your attendance initiative into existing curriculum or lesson plans for a variety of subjects. Examples of how to do this are provided later in this chapter.

Determine When to Provide General Lessons that Emphasize Attendance

Plan to periodically teach specific lessons throughout the year about the importance of attendance and being on time. These lessons may involve activities such as brainstorming the negative effects of missing school on individual students and the classroom as a whole and having students calculate or visually depict the number of days of absence that would place them in the regular, at-risk, chronic, or severe chronic absence categories within a term and within a school year. We suggest you start the school year with several of these lessons that clearly illustrate for students that regular attendance is a primary goal in your class and critical for the success of individual students and the functioning of the class as a whole. For middle and high school teachers, plan to provide this information at the beginning of each quarter/semester with each new group and provide reminder lessons for any year-long classes.

Also, consider when during the day/period to deliver attendance lessons. You may be tempted to teach lessons at the beginning of the day after taking attendance. However, if you frequently have students who are tardy, it may be beneficial to wait until the end of the day or period, when more students are present. Students who are frequently tardy are likely to be students who most need to hear the messages within your attendance lessons! In secondary school, these lessons might be appropriate with an advisory-type group; however, if absenteeism issues are problematic in your school, it may be necessary to consider ways to provide abbreviated lessons for all your classes, frequently mention the importance of attendance, and incorporate positive attendance messages into your subject-matter teaching. Examples of how to weave attendance messaging into subject-area lessons are at the end of this chapter.

Use Classroom Attendance Data to Guide Lesson Planning

Your classroom attendance data can be a valuable tool to inform instructional decision making around attendance for your classroom. Attendance data can be used to identify trends in absenteeism for your students, such as when absenteeism is most prevalent (e.g., by day of week, time of day, or time of year). These trends can then be used to create specific lessons. For example, when reviewing your classroom data, you may notice a trend that absenteeism increased on days when you let your class know that you would be gone (e.g., when planning to attend a professional development opportunity). In this case, you would want to address this trend by reteaching the importance of attendance prior to any preplanned absence and emphasizing the academic work and learning that will be accomplished while you are gone. Of course, this would also need to be paired with lesson plans for subs that have instructional value!

Other collected data, as described in Chapter 2, can help you determine lessons that may be beneficial to address common barriers to attendance and other causes. For example, one teacher shared with us that many students in her class lacked strong morning routines for getting ready for school, which resulted in them missing the bus, making a parent late for work, or coming in late to class. She worked to teach explicit lessons to her whole class on how to set an effective morning routine that would eliminate these concerns. Another teacher found that many students had parents who worked early in the morning or who were otherwise unable to help wake her students up for school. She worked with her students on explicit skills, like how to set an alarm clock and get ready on their own. A survey, class discussion, or reflection writing activity can help you determine common reasons students in your class are coming late or missing class. (See Chapter 2 for ways to collect data to determine common causes of absenteeism.) You may also gather information from parents through a survey or other communication that can guide your decision making about what lessons may be beneficial for students.

(See Chapter 5 for strategies for collaborating with parents to determine and address causes of absenteeism.)

Data from the previous year can also be used to determine lessons to address time-of-year trends. For example, if you notice that absenteeism predictably spikes directly before the winter vacation, consider what lessons can be developed to emphasize that there will be valuable instruction occurring during these weeks and tailor your instructional plans for those weeks accordingly. If there is a time of year when illnesses, such as colds or the flu, are likely, plan to provide lessons on the importance of hand washing (and how to wash hands to prevent illness) and why students should not pass food or drink items back and forth with peers.

Also explore the data to determine if there are trends that explain days or weeks when students have perfect attendance. Are there positive trends associated with specific events in your classroom? For instance, do all students show up on days when the school counselor comes to your room for social-emotional lessons, days with pep rallies, or days when students know they have earned a class reward, such as a class party? If you can identify these trends, you can use these events to try to increase attendance, especially during problematic times of year. For example, you might let your class know that there will be a class party sometime the following week, but randomly select the day of the party. Or, have the counselor come for social-emotional lessons on an unpredictable schedule, and have him stop by for a few minutes to reinforce students on days when all students in the class are present.

Lesson Ideas

Figures 4.1, 4.2, and 4.3 provide sample lesson plans for different grade levels. In addition, consider whether lessons on any of the following topics would be beneficial in your class(es):

- Why is attendance important? Brainstorming negative effects of absenteeism on a student, class, and parents
- Regular attendance is the goal—what does that mean?
- Learning is harder when you miss classes here and there throughout the year
- Late start/early release days are still school days!
- How to stay healthy during cold and flu season
- Strategies for problem solving bullying situations

- Strategies for problem solving conflict with peers or adults at school
- Troubleshooting transportation difficulties (e.g., missing the bus, parents always running late, long distance to walk to school or bus stop)
- How to communicate with a staff member about situations that make you feel unsafe on your way to school or at school
- How to advocate for oneself about being at school every day (e.g., when a parent wants to take a vacation, when scheduling medical or dental appointments, when being asked to babysit siblings)
- Coping strategies for a change in routine or anxiety about aspects of school (e.g., testing)
- How to enter the classroom if tardy so that instruction can continue
- How to get missed assignments and stay on top of learning if you are seriously ill or need to legitimately miss class
- How to access clothing, school supplies, or other needed materials (e.g., laundry machines) if financial issues make it difficult to attend school

Design Focused, Interactive Attendance Lessons

Design Lessons to Teach Specific Skills

Some lessons require you to teach students specific skills to increase attendance in your classroom (e.g., setting an alarm clock, using a checklist for evening and morning routines, using an assignment log to monitor assignments, managing anxiety with deep breathing or other relaxation skills). When teaching a specific skill, use principles of effective instruction and consider prerequisite skills and how the skill will need to be broken down and logically sequenced for the age, developmental level(s), and skill level(s) of your students. For example, if you are teaching students how to set a digital alarm clock, they will need to be able to learn how to set the time on the clock and then set the alarm. Prerequisite skills include reading numerals 1–12 for the hour and 00–59 for the minute, and knowing the difference between a.m. and p.m. and how to read a digital display on the clock. A logical sequence of instruction would involve using the model, lead, and test structure (explained later in this section) for each of the following steps:

1. Practice reading time on a digital clock.
2. Set the time on the alarm clock.
3. Check the time.
4. Set the alarm.

FIGURE 4.1 **Trouble at School (Grades K–2)**

Materials

- Copy of the book or video *Berenstain Bears' Trouble at School* by Stan and Jan Berenstain (www.youtube.com/watch?v=clC7PLw2zEU)

Step 1: Gain Students' Attention

We know how important school is. Our goal is to be in school every day.

Objectives

- Students identify why Brother Bear had trouble when he came back to school after being sick.
- Students will discuss how missing school impacts learning.
- Students will identify ways Brother Bear could avoid these problems in the future.

Step 2: State the Goal of the Lesson and Its Relevance

Today we are going to watch/read *Berenstain Bears' Trouble at School* by Stan and Jan Berenstain. In this book, Brother Bear stays home from school when he is sick and then has trouble when he comes back to school. Our goal is to identify what made it difficult for Brother Bear to come back after being absent and how he could avoid these problems in the future.

Step 3: Procedures

a. Read aloud *Berenstain Bears' Trouble at School* (or watch the video). As you proceed, ask questions to check for student understanding.
b. When finished, review each major section of the book/video and have students discuss the following questions with a partner:
   i. Why did Brother Bear stay home from school? Was this an OK reason to miss school?
   ii. When Brother Bear returned to school, what problems did he have? Why?
   iii. What could Brother Bear do differently next time?

(continued)

FIGURE 4.1 **Trouble at School (Grades K–2)** *(continued)*

Step 3: Procedures
c. For each question, have a group discussion and ask for pairs to share their responses. As you proceed, emphasize that missing school means missing new information, opportunities to learn and practice new things, and work with your team and friends.
Step 4: Review/Close the Lesson
Review with the class that their learning relies on them being in class every day when they are not seriously ill. Also explain that when they are absent, it is important for them to work on what they can at home and work with you, the teacher, to get caught up when they return.

FIGURE 4.2 **Missing School Makes Learning Harder (Grades 3–5)**

Objective
• Students will reflect on and discuss how missing school can lead to gaps in critical knowledge.
Materials
• Each student will need 10 to 20 manipulatives (math blocks with multiple colors to make a pattern). • Each student will need a "Missing School Makes Learning Harder" worksheet.
Step 1: Gain Students' Attention
We know how important school is. Our goal is to be in school every day.
Step 2: State the Goal of the Lesson and Its Relevance
Today we are going to participate in an experiment on learning. This experiment will have three trials, and after each trial you will rate how successful you felt as the learner.
Step 3: Procedures
1. Distribute materials to all students. 2. Trial 1 (three minutes) a. Teacher models for the students each step in building a pattern with their blocks. b. Students build the pattern with their blocks. c. Students compare their patterns with the teacher's model. d. Students rate how successful they felt as a learner. 3. Trial 2 (three minutes) a. Teacher models the first part of the pattern but, partway through the instruction, stops modeling and shares a completed version. Compare this trial to leaving school early. The pattern should be complex enough that it will be difficult for students to figure out the pattern on their own. b. Students build the pattern with their blocks.

(continued)

FIGURE 4.2 **Missing School Makes Learning Harder (Grades 3–5)** *(continued)*

3. Trial 2 (three minutes) *continued*
   c. Students compare their patterns with the teacher model.
   d. Students rate how successful they felt as a learner.
4. Trial 3 (three minutes)
   a. Teacher has a model already completed with a very complex pattern. Students receive no instruction and are asked to build the pattern with their blocks. Compare this trial to missing the whole day.
   b. Students build the pattern with their blocks.
   c. Students compare their patterns with the teacher model.
   d. Students rate how successful they felt as a learner.
5. Have students do a think-pair-share on how they felt during the different parts of the activity. (nine minutes)
   a. Think: Have students rate: I felt like I was successful, I struggled with this task but was able to complete it, I was unable to complete the task.

      Have them complete the sentence starters: I felt successful in Trial(s) _______ because __________. I learn best and can most easily complete all the tasks when I __________________. (three minutes)
   b. Pair: Have students share their responses with a partner from the same group. (three minutes)
   c. Share: Each group shares their responses. (three minutes)
6. Have students reflect and discuss how the task was easier/more challenging for the different trials. Compare the first trial to being in school every day and having good attendance, the second trial to coming in late/leaving early, and the third trial to missing school for a day. Explain how it is more difficult to learn when you aren't there for the initial instruction.
   a. Provide one or two examples: "When you miss instruction, you may miss important information, such as a new math concept. Just like it was difficult for you to complete the pattern, math may be more difficult for you if you aren't here every day."
   b. Have students talk in their groups about how this experiment relates to attendance in school. Have them generate ideas on the importance of being in school every day.
   c. Have students share with the whole class responses that relate to school attendance and explain why.

Missing School Makes Learning Harder Worksheet
Check how you felt as a learner in each of the trials. Trial 1: ❑ I easily completed the task. ❑ I struggled with this task but was able to complete it. ❑ I was unable to complete the task. Trial 2: ❑ I easily completed the task. ❑ I struggled with this task but was able to complete it. ❑ I was unable to complete the task. Trial 3: ❑ I easily completed the task. ❑ I struggled with this task but was able to complete it. ❑ I was unable to complete the task. Complete the following sentences: I felt successful in Trial(s)____________ because ____________________ ____ ____ ____. I learn best and can most easily complete all the tasks when I ____________ ____ ____ ____.
Step 4: Review/Close the Lesson
Review with the class that their learning relies on them being in class every day.

Teacher may modify lessons to make them age appropriate.

FIGURE 4.3 **Shortened-Day Lesson (Middle/High School Grades)**

Objective
• Students will explain why it is important for them to attend school on early release/late start days.
Materials
• Academic schedule for shortened day • School calendar • Letter to parent/guardian • Think-Pair-Share Worksheet
Step 1: Gain Students' Attention
School is incredibly important. Every minute of every day counts.
Step 2: State the Goal of the Lesson and Its Relevance
Today we are going to discuss how learning still occurs on shortened days and how important it is that you are here every day, even on shortened days. During the last few shortened days there has been a decrease in attendance, and we need to change that!
Step 3: Procedures
1. On a slide, show the class the shortened day schedule of academics. 2. Have students identify the minutes devoted to each subject/period on shortened days and total instructional minutes across the day. a. English LA = 28 minutes b. Math = 28 minutes c. Science = 28 minutes d. Etc. e. Total = 196 minutes = 3.26 hours 3. Have students calculate the difference in minutes between a "typical" day and a shortened day.

4. Have students do a think-pair-share for how "typical" days are different from and the same as shortened days.
   a. Think: Have students write how the "typical" days are different from shortened days.

   Have them write how "typical" days are the same as shortened days. Then have them identify why it is important to attend every day.

   b. Pair: Have students share their responses with a partner.

   c. Share: Randomly select students to share their partner's responses.
5. Reinforce to students that learning will still occur on shortened days.
6. Explain to the class that they will now calculate the total days if a student missed every shortened day.
7. Have students use a school calendar to calculate how many shortened days there are in the year. Have students put their thumbs up when they know the total number of shortened days.
8. With the total number of shortened days, share with the students the total number of calendar days and have students come up with a percentage (180 school days, 18 shortened days = 10% of total days).
9. Have students do a think-pair-share on students who miss all shortened days. Which category of attendance would they fall in (regular attenders, at-risk attenders, chronic absenteeism, severely chronic absenteeism), and how might this impact them academically?
10. Share with the class how missing 10% or more of school puts them at higher risk of dropping out of school.
11. Privately share with each student his or her personal attendance rate for shortened days and have each student set a goal for the remainder of the year.
12. Send home a letter to the parent/guardian with the child's goal for shortened day attendance.

(continued)

FIGURE 4.3 **Shortened-Day Lesson (Middle/High School Grades)** *(continued)*

Think-Pair-Share Worksheet

Think-Pair-Share		
How are "typical" days different from shortened days?		
How are "typical" days the same as shortened days?		
Why is it important to attend every day?		
Total shortened days:	Total school days:	Percentage of shortened days:
Missing all shortened days would put a student into which category?	___ regular attendance ___ at-risk attendance ___ chronic absence ___ severely chronic absence	
Set your goal for attending on shortened days.		

Step 4: Review/Close the Lesson

Review with the class that their learning relies on them being in class every day. Shortened days are still important educational days. Learning will occur, and students must be present to learn!

Spartan Spirit

DEDICATED TO ACADEMIC EXCELLENCE

Letter to Parent/Guardian

Dear Parent/Guardian,

This year our school has many shortened days on our calendars. These days are still important for your student to attend, as learning will still occur. Out of our 180-day school year, our school has 18 shortened days. That's 10% of our school days.

During these shortened days, students still receive 28 minutes of instruction in each class period, which is over three hours of academic instruction. Your student and the class as a whole can make valuable progress on these days—so it is important that your student is here, ready to learn.

If your student missed every shortened day, they would already be in the chronically absent category—without even getting sick! We know that missing 10% or more of school is associated with lower academic performance and increased risk of dropping out of school.

Your student has already set the goal to be at school for every shortened day. Let's help all of our students achieve this important goal!

Effective lessons are designed using best-practice instructional principles. This involves doing more than just lecturing students on the importance of attendance—it requires helping students draw on their own experiences so they can understand the "why" in developmentally and contextually relevant terms. Lessons can take many formats, such as stories or chants, lectures with active participation, modeling, t-charts, role play, analogous problems, and discussions. Each attendance lesson should have a specific focus and goal and use techniques common to good instruction. Before you begin to develop a lesson, consider what your students already know and what you want them to learn. Then make instructional decisions about how to incorporate each of the following features:

Provide a rationale/goal. Provide the "why" of the lesson. This will help you articulate the goals for the lesson and intended outcomes to your students, administrators, parents, and other stakeholders.

Post objectives for the lesson. Learning objectives are the backbone for developing your lesson plan. They clarify the intent and purpose of instruction and how instruction relates to the rationale/goal. Objectives should describe in precise, measurable terms what learners will be able to do at the end of the lesson or unit. A well-written behavioral objective includes three components: a statement of condition, a behavioral verb, and criteria for performance (e.g., All students will communicate verbally or in writing at least five reasons why it is important to attend school every day they are not seriously ill).

Use a model, lead, and test structure (Archer & Hughes, 2011). In this structure, model a positive example or response, provide students with an opportunity to practice with your guidance, and then check for their independent understanding. Modeling consists of two main components: demonstrating the skill and describing what is being done. The number of demonstrations performed by you will depend on the complexity of the skill, your students' ability to learn new skills, their background knowledge, and the time you have available.

Leading the class involves guiding students through the problem or concept together. Incorporate prompts such as directions, clues, and reminders about what to do when performing a skill. As students are successful with responses, fade prompts so they occur less often, until you determine students are ready for an independent test of their abilities. In general, guided practice will take the majority of the time in an instructional sequence.

Testing the class occurs when you check each student's individual understanding or mastery of the content. Check if students can perform the skill or demonstrate knowledge without any prompts from you or peers.

The following example applies model, lead, and test to a lesson on the importance of attendance:

- Model: Teacher explains three reasons why it is important to come to class every day.
- Lead: Students share three to five reasons why it is important to come to class.
- Test: Students individually write their three reasons.

Use Active Engagement Strategies Throughout Instruction

To engage students and help them stay focused on what is being taught, incorporate active engagement strategies. Active engagement strategies have students pose and respond to questions, process new information, manipulate information, and relate new learning to what they already know.

A central component of active engagement is providing all students with frequent opportunities to respond (OTRs) throughout instruction. OTRs are instructional questions, statements, or gestures made by the teacher that seek an academic response from students (Sprick, Knight, Reinke, Skyles, & Barnes, 2010). OTRs may include verbal responses such as choral response, written responses such as drawing or writing an answer to a question, and action responses such as making a gesture to represent a concept or physically role playing. These responses may be performed by individual students, partners or small groups, or a whole class. In general, work to incorporate OTRs that require all students to participate, rather than relying on procedures like calling on volunteers, which demonstrates only one student's understanding. For example, prior to having students share out loud as part of whole-class discussion, have them share in partner groups.

The following are examples of OTRs (Archer & Hughes, 2011; detailed discussion):

- Choral response
- Think-pair-share
- Partner or group discussion
- Cloze note writing (i.e., using partially completed notes and filling in the blanks)

- Randomly selected individual student response
- Holding up whiteboards with written responses or drawings
- Holding up response cards (e.g., "yes/no," multiple choice: "a, b, c, d")
- Signaling (e.g., thumbs up/thumbs down, showing one to five fingers to signal levels of understanding or agreement)
- Role play

As you implement OTRs throughout instruction, carefully consider strategies for how to ask the class questions, manage student responses, and provide positive and corrective feedback in ways that increase the likelihood of active and desired responses in the future. Providing students with opportunities to respond has many proven benefits, including increasing on-task behavior, increasing students' ability to retrieve information quickly, and decreasing disruptive behavior (Brophy, 1986; Shores, Gunter, & Jack, 1993; Sutherland, Lewis-Palmer, Stichter, & Morgan, 2008).

Provide Opportunities for Repeated Practice

Repeated practice opportunities are not the same as rote repetition. The goal is to provide enough practice that students can improve their performance and understanding and acquire mastery on the content and automaticity. Automaticity occurs when students can apply knowledge automatically without reflection. Provide opportunities for repeated practice as often as necessary to ensure that students can meet your instructional goals and lesson objectives. For example, incorporate the importance of attendance as a bellringer where students are pushed to generate additional reasons why it is important to attend school every day.

Assess All Students' Understanding and Provide Feedback

Checking for understanding is an important part of any lesson and includes both ongoing formative assessment of understanding and summative assessment at the end of a unit of linked concepts. This allows you to know exactly what students are getting out of the lesson and unit and helps you identify any students who are struggling with particular aspects of the learning. Frequent checks for understanding also allow you to provide specific and effective positive and corrective feedback to help students meet instructional goals. Feedback should be as specific as possible, letting them know exactly what they did well, what may still need improvement, or what they are doing differently than before (Hattie & Timperley, 2007). For example, as a student reviews her personal attendance graph and notices an upward trend, the teacher might provide positive feedback like, "I've noticed that your attendance has really improved. You have been coming to school more often in the last month, which is changing your trend line. This is going to help you reach your attendance goal."

Incorporate Attendance Messages into Content Lessons

In addition to creating your own lessons that address trends/barriers to attendance specific to your classroom, consider ways to incorporate an attendance message into your already existing curriculum units. In English, you may incorporate the dependability of the main characters of a story and discuss how the story would be different if the main character didn't show up for a major scene. A few ideas for different content areas are:

- In health class, provide lessons connecting hygiene and healthy lifestyle choices to attendance patterns in school and work.
- In English or Language Arts, have students write sentences, paragraphs, or persuasive essays on why attendance is important.
- In math, have students work with the school's data or other data from attendance studies when learning about graphing, percentages, statistics, and other related mathematical concepts.
- In finance or math, have students calculate the hourly pay for a variety of jobs, then calculate lost wages based on days absent or hours late.
- In social studies or history, discuss what would have happened if historical figures had not shown up on a historical day of importance (for example, the signing of the Constitution).
- In science, during lessons on plant growth, have students discuss or experiment with how attending or not attending to plants would impact the growth of the plants, and compare this to student growth in school.

See Figure 4.4 for additional examples of potential lesson topics for several of the Common Core State Standards in mathematics and reading.

FIGURE 4.4 Potential Lesson Topics: Common Core State Standards, Mathematics and Reading

Common Core State Standard–Mathematics	Attendance Lesson Ideas
• CCSS.MATH.CONTENT.K.MD.A.2 Directly compare two objects with a measurable attribute in common to see which object has more/less of the attribute and describe the difference. *For example, directly compare the heights of two children and describe one child as taller/shorter.*	Keep track of daily attendance in your classroom, and each day have students talk about whether "more" or "less" students are present than the day before. Compete with another kindergarten classroom and compare weekly averages to determine which class has "more" or "less" students coming to school.
• CCSS.MATH.CONTENT.2.MD.C.7 Tell and write time from analog and digital clocks to the nearest five minutes, using a.m. and p.m.	Teach students how to tell and write time and also how to set an alarm clock so that they can wake up and come to school on time. Discuss the importance of being able to read time so that students can be dependable at school.
• CCSS.MATH.CONTENT.4.NF.B.3.A Understand addition and subtraction of fractions as joining and separating parts referring to the same whole.	Use fractions for days present versus days absent out of total days available.
• CCSS.MATH.CONTENT.4.OA.A.3 Solve multistep word problems posed with whole numbers and having whole-number answers using the four operations, including problems in which remainders must be interpreted. Represent these problems using equations with a letter standing for the unknown quantity. Assess the reasonableness of answers using mental computation and estimation strategies including rounding.	Provide students with a worksheet where they solve word problems around attendance issues. For instance, if a student attends 136 days out of 142 possible days, how many days did the student miss? School has been in session for 98 days, and Charlie has missed five days. How many days has he attended?

Common Core State Standard–Mathematics	Attendance Lesson Ideas
• CCSS.MATH.CONTENT.6.RP.A.1 Understand the concept of a ratio and use ratio language to describe a ratio relationship between two quantities. *For example, "The ratio of wings to beaks in the birdhouse at the zoo was 2:1, because for every two wings, there was one beak." "For every vote candidate A received, candidate C received nearly three votes."*	Develop a ratio for the following scenario: For every one student who is chronically absent, there are five students who are regular attenders. The ratio of students who are chronically absent to students who are regular attenders is 1:5, because for every one student who was chronically absent, there were five students who were regular attenders.
• CCSS.MATH.CONTENT.7.SP.A.1 Understand that statistics can be used to gain information about a population by examining a sample of the population; generalizations about a population from a sample are valid only if the sample is representative of that population. Understand that random sampling tends to produce representative samples and support valid inferences.	Have students pull a sample from the schoolwide attendance data (e.g., 7th grade homeroom attendance) and then compare it to the data of the whole school. Have students discuss how the sample was or was not representative of the population and why. Then have students randomly select four classrooms from the school, compare this random sample to the schoolwide data, and discuss how a larger random sample changed the comparison to the population.
• CCSS.MATH.CONTENT.8.SP.A.1 Construct and interpret scatter plots for bivariate measurement data to investigate patterns of association between two quantities. Describe patterns, such as clustering, outliers, positive or negative association, linear association, and nonlinear association.	Have students look at de-identified student attendance data and academic data. Have students describe the patterns between the two quantities (e.g., the more days students attend, the higher the academic outcomes, which means there is a positive association between attendance and academic outcomes).
• CCSS.MATH.CONTENT.HSS.IC.A.1 Understand statistics as a process for making inferences about population parameters based on a random sample from that population.	Have students randomly choose several classes, gather their attendance data, and use that data to make an inference on school-level data. If available, students could randomly choose schools within the district to predict district-level attendance.

(continued)

FIGURE 4.4 Potential Lesson Topics: Common Core State Standards, Mathematics and Reading *(continued)*

Common Core State Standard-English Language Arts—Reading	Attendance Lesson Ideas
• CCSS.ELA-LITERACY.RL.K.9 With prompting and support, compare and contrast the adventures and experiences of characters in familiar stories.	In a book with one character who shows grit and one who does not, have students compare these two characters' adventures and experiences. Discuss how attending school every day builds the ability to work hard toward a goal. Example: *The Little Engine That Could* by Watty Piper
• CCSS.ELA-LITERACY.RL.1.2 Retell stories, including key details, and demonstrate understanding of their central message or lesson.	Use a book that illustrates the importance of being dependable, such as *Horton Hears A Who* by Dr. Seuss. Extend the lesson by having students discuss what might have happened if Horton was not dependable. Have students discuss how showing up to school every day demonstrates dependability and how their peers need them there for group work.
• CCSS.ELA-LITERACY.RL.2.3 Describe how characters in a story respond to major events and challenges.	Use a book that illustrates the importance of teamwork and being there for each other, such as *Toad and Frog Together* by Arnold Lobel. Extend the lesson to discuss how the story would be different if the characters were not dependable. Have students discuss the importance of being in school every day for partner work.
• CCSS.ELA-LITERACY.RL.3.2 Recount stories—including fables, folktales, and myths from diverse cultures—and determine the central message, lesson, or moral. Explain how it is conveyed through key details in the text.	Choose a story that centers around perseverance, such as *The Tortoise and the Hare* by Aesop. Have students discuss how the tortoise never gave up and tried his hardest throughout the race, which is like coming to school every day to learn new knowledge. School is their race, and to win, they must be there every day.

Common Core State Standard-English Language Arts Reading	Attendance Lesson Ideas
• CCSS.ELA-LITERACY.RL.4.3 Describe in depth a character, setting, or event in a story or drama, drawing on specific details in the text (e.g., a character's thoughts, words, or actions).	Choose a character who shows the trait of perseverance or dependability, such as Charlotte in *Charlotte's Web* by E. B. White. Have students describe the character in depth and the importance of her being there every day for Wilbur. Have students extend this by comparing it to the importance of being in school every day.
• CCSS.ELA-LITERACY.RL.5.3 Compare two or more characters, settings, or events in a story or drama, drawing on specific details in the text (e.g., how characters interact).	Identify two characters in a book, such as *Wonder* by R. J. Palacio, who interact with the main character. Discuss how these interactions made the main character feel and which characteristics meant the most to Auggie. Have students extend this by comparing these traits to those that are necessary to be successful in school (and life), such as dependability, resilience, and kindness.

■ ■ ■ ■ ■

Many students may have never been formally taught the importance of regular attendance and do not understand that missing school on occasion can have a big impact on their academic and social goals. If we want to increase attendance in our classrooms, we must teach our students about the importance of attending school every day and provide them with the skills they need to increase their attendance. Formal classroom lessons, as described in this chapter, can go a long way toward providing that awareness, understanding, and skill. The next chapter provides information about how to involve parents and other stakeholders as partners in the process of building a culture of attendance for your students.

Summary of Chapter 4 Tasks

Teach lessons about attendance to all students. Determine a list of topics for lessons and/or ways to incorporate attendance lessons into existing units of instruction (see p. 67 for lesson ideas). Develop a schedule for when lessons will be delivered:

- Determine when to provide general lessons that emphasize attendance.
- Determine when to provide specific lessons based on attendance data and trends (e.g., handwashing during cold and flu season).

Create lessons using principles for effective instruction, such as:

- Provide a rationale/goal.
- Post objectives for the lesson.
- Use a model, lead, and test structure.
- Use active engagement strategies throughout instruction.
- Provide opportunities for repeated practice.
- Assess all students' understanding and provide feedback.

5

Partnering with Families

Absenteeism is not a problem that a classroom teacher, or even a whole school, can tackle alone. Family members play a critical role in whether a student has the supports needed and the motivation to attend school on a regular basis. As you are the front line of communication with families, you play a critical role in connecting and partnering with families to improve student attendance. However, we know that making and maintaining these connections can be a potentially overwhelming and time-intensive endeavor. With that in mind, we provide tools in this chapter for educating families about the importance of attendance and realistic ways to facilitate collaboration and positive involvement with even the most difficult-to-reach parents.

Communicate About Attendance Goals and Data

It is easy to think that there is little we can do as educators to effect change with our parent population. We sometimes hear educators make statements like this: "We can't do anything to change his attendance. It's a parent problem, and his parents just don't care about school or his regular attendance." However, although very few families may truly not care, the good news is that a far greater number are simply operating off misinformation or don't have adequate tools, skills, and supports to help their student attend school regularly. This is where regular communication about attendance goals and data can play a critical role in dispelling parent misconceptions and help them understand that their student must attend school every day when not seriously ill. Parents should receive regular communication that includes overall information about your attendance initiative and classroom data, as well as specific information about their child's attendance. The goal is to ensure that parents know exactly how many absences their child has accrued at any point during the school year—and the corresponding attendance category.

Provide Information on the Initiative in a Variety of Formats

As you begin your attendance initiative, consider using multiple formats and methods for connecting with families to increase the likelihood that parents understand the importance of attendance and your goals. Make sure to emphasize the goal of regular attendance (missing 5 percent or fewer days) and communicate that you would like to be a partner in problem solving with any family that has difficulty meeting this goal. Strive to make all communication about your initiative informative, welcoming, and nonjudgmental. Acknowledge that while you understand there can be significant barriers to regular attendance, regular attendance is so critical to your students' success and the efficacy of your classroom that you will continuously strive to help your students maintain regular attendance.

As much as possible, provide information and materials in families' first languages and invite interpreters to events that parents will attend. Select from the following menu of ways to communicate with parents, or design your own activities and communication to get parents involved.

Prepare a Brief Presentation About the Importance of Attendance at Back-to-School Night

Consider ways to best communicate your attendance goals with parents. You might pull relevant information from Chapter 1 on the negative effects of absenteeism to share with families and also share anecdotal notes from previous years about how absenteeism has negatively affected your classroom. During this time, you can teach parents how to use the attendance chart (see Chapter 3) or provide other tips and tools for improving attendance as described later in this chapter.

Blast Information via Social Media

If you have a classroom social media account that parents follow, send out communications that provide important information and generate enthusiasm (e.g., "In two days, Mrs. Johnson's science students will be launching a new campaign that may be the biggest thing yet for helping our students be successful. Stay tuned!")

Publish a Regular Story in Your Classroom Newsletter

If you have a classroom newsletter, dedicate a regular space for an attendance column. In this space, you can continue to emphasize the importance of attendance and class goals (e.g., "Our goal is to have a 97 percent average daily attendance rate"), share classroom-level attendance data (e.g., "We have been maintaining a 94 percent average daily attendance rate"), and provide information about any classroom efforts to improve attendance (e.g., "To try to reach our goals, we will be launching a classroom motivational system where the whole group will work together to earn rewards based on improved attendance"). Ensure that any classroom-level data that you share do not single out any student or group of students that struggles with attendance.

Send Home Color-Coded Letters Indicating Each Student's Attendance Rate

Create form letters that can be sent home at least every two months to indicate a student's attendance category (regular attendance, at-risk attendance, chronic absence, or severe chronic absence). Print each letter on colored paper that signifies the level of risk (e.g., green for regular, yellow for at-risk, red for chronic, dark red for severe chronic), and tailor the message accordingly. (See Figures 5.1 and 5.2 for sample wording for a regular attendance letter and a chronic absence letter, respectively.) To increase the value of this letter, have each student fill in the number of absences and their attendance percentage on a separate sheet of paper (that is not color-coded and therefore does not embarrass the student). Then have the student sign it, and you can add it to the color-coded letter before it is sent home.

FIGURE 5.1 **Parent Letter for Regular Attendance**

Spartan
Spirit

DEDICATED TO ACADEMIC EXCELLENCE

Dear Parent/Guardian of ____________________:

I want to congratulate you and your student for maintaining regular attendance (missing no more than 5 percent of days in the current year)! So far this year, your student has had ________ absences, representing an attendance rate of ________ percent. I know that it is not always easy to get to school each day, and I truly appreciate your efforts to set your student up for success. You are also helping the class reach our goal of 97 percent Average Daily Attendance. Keep up the good work!

Research shows that students who miss even a few days each month are at far greater risk of academic failure and dropping out than students who attend regularly. By ensuring that your student has fewer than nine absences in a year, you are helping your student have the best chances in life. If there are difficulties that may make your student miss too much school, please feel free to contact me or the school counselor, Joan Ndogo, at 555-1234 for assistance. We are happy to work with you to help your student maintain regular attendance.

Sincerely,

Mr. Allan

2nd Grade Teacher, Room 212

FIGURE 5.2 **Parent Letter for Chronic Absence**

Spartan Spirit

DEDICATED TO ACADEMIC EXCELLENCE

Dear Parent/Guardian of ____________________:

I want to connect with you about your student's current attendance rate and reach out to see how we can partner to help your student maintain regular attendance. So far this year, your student has had ________ absences, representing an attendance rate of _________ percent.

Research shows that students who miss even a few days each month are at far greater risk of academic failure and dropping out than students who attend regularly, so your student's current attendance rate triggers some concern. Students who miss 10 percent or more of school often have difficulty with academic content, struggle to maintain positive relationships with peers or adults in the school, and have higher rates of disengagement and school failure over time than students with regular attendance.

I know that it is not always easy to get to school each day—after all, I'm a parent too! Many situations can cause a student to be absent from school. However, I also know that with a partnership between the school and families, we can work together to find solutions to many of the barriers and situations that prevent students from being in school. Please contact me or the school counselor, Joan Ndogo, at 555-1234. We are happy to work with you to help your student maintain regular attendance. If we do not hear from you and attendance continues to be a concern, we will be in touch to problem solve and work out a plan.

I want to sincerely thank you for your efforts to help your student attend school regularly. By working to ensure your student is in school every day when not seriously ill, you are helping your student have the best chances in school and in life.

Sincerely,

Mr. Allan

2nd Grade Teacher, Room 212

Make Student Attendance a Standard Talking Point During Parent-Teacher Conferences

Conferences are a great opportunity to remind parents about the importance of regular attendance for their students and the class community. Prior to conferences, create a form letter similar to those depicted in Figures 5.1 and 5.2, and place the appropriate letters in student files before conferences. Following are recommendations for conducting these conversations:

- Congratulate parents of students with regular attendance and encourage them to keep getting their students to school regularly. Remind them that the fewer absences their child has during a year, the greater the likelihood of success. They are giving their students a foundation that supports success.
- Let parents of students with at-risk attendance know that the student's attendance is below what is recommended for the student to have the best possible chances of success in school. Say, for example:

  Johnny has missed five days in the first three months of school, which puts him in the at-risk attendance category. We know that students in this category may experience negative outcomes if absenteeism continues, such as lower grades, disengagement from adults or peers, and other struggles in school.

  Ask parents if there is anything they need help with or any way the school can help in getting the student to school. Provide contact information for personnel in the school who can assist if parents need support. Say, for example:

  We know that it's not always easy getting to school each day and that many families face barriers that may prevent a student from being in school. If you have any of these concerns and would like to talk to me or someone else at the school, we hope to assist in any way we can. If you would like to get in touch with someone, here is my e-mail address. We've also included the phone numbers and e-mail addresses of our counselor and social worker in this letter.

  Conclude this portion of the conference by indicating that you look forward to having the student in class every day.

- With parents of students who are chronically or severely chronically absent, attempt to strike a supportive and nonjudgmental tone, but indicate that the student's absences are a concern. For example:

  Cinda and Darrell, I've noticed that Martin has missed seven days of school in the first three months, which means he has been chronically absent. In education, we are very concerned when a student misses this much school because there are significant risks, such as course failure, disengagement, and dropping out. I also miss him when he is absent, and so do his peers! I would love to work with you to problem solve and figure out the best way to improve his attendance.

  Highlight the information about personnel in the school who are available to provide support and who will be in touch if absenteeism continues to be a problem. For example:

  I know that it's not always easy getting to school each day and that many families face barriers that may prevent a student from being in school. If you would like to talk to me or someone else at the school about any concerns that make it difficult for Martin to attend regularly, we hope to assist in any way we can. If you would like to get in touch with someone, here is my e-mail address. I've also included the phone numbers and e-mail addresses of our counselor and social worker in this letter. Please know that we view Martin's attendance as a critical factor in his success and that if the current attendance pattern continues and we haven't heard from you, we will follow up with you and with Martin to see what we can all do to solve this issue.

Provide Strategies for Addressing Common Issues that Contribute to Absenteeism

Many parents would do more to support our school efforts if we could make them aware of specific problems, and even better, provide tools and strategies to support their involvement. Communicating with families to address widespread issues in your classroom can help decrease the number of students who continue to experience attendance problems. Use the full range of methods available (e.g., back-to-school nights, letters home, social media, a classroom newsletter) to communicate concerns about common issues and convey recommended strategies for supporting students and addressing those concerns. The following are examples of possible approaches.

Provide Tips on Technology and Social Media Use

Do you have students who miss school because they have been staying up too late playing video games, texting, or using social media? Or do some students miss school because of cyberbullying that occurs outside of school when many students are not supervised in their use of technology? Many problems that relate to absenteeism may originate from inadequately structured and supervised technology use at home. See Appendix B for "Dealing with Technology: Tips and Strategies for Families," a handout that offers strategies for setting expectations and rules regarding technology use, teaching responsible digital citizenship, and providing supervision.

Educate Families on Sickness (How Sick Is Too Sick?)

Although illness is the leading reported cause of absenteeism, many excused absences for illness are for minor conditions that are not serious enough to warrant remaining home from school. Some excused absences for illness may also occur when a student is experiencing anxiety or simply wants to be with a family member or to do things that reinforce the desire to stay home, such as playing video games or watching movies. The student may express physical concerns (e.g., a headache or stomachache) to an adult caregiver when other symptoms are absent. While we are not medical professionals, we have created the sample handout titled "How Sick Is Too Sick for School?" (see Appendix B), which includes some basic information to help parents determine if a child who is complaining of illness should stay home or go to school. When a parent answers "no" to each item on the checklist, the student is probably healthy enough to attend school. Have your school or district nursing staff review and adapt the checklist or develop one for your school. It may be beneficial to teach one or more lessons to students on how to use the checklist. Lessons should cover things like appropriate and inappropriate times to miss school. Redistribute this form and emphasize the contents with families and students at times of the year with increased illnesses (e.g., flu or allergy season).

Provide Tips for Improving Students' Sleep Habits

Many students miss school because they are not getting enough sleep and are overly tired, or they get sick because their immune system is weakened. "Tips for Improving Your Child's Sleep and Reducing Absenteeism" in Appendix B, while not intended to be medical advice, provides some basic sleep tips that could be sent home to parents in a newsletter or e-mail blast, or taught during a back-to-school or parent night. It may also be useful to teach one or more lessons to students on how to get the recommended amount of sleep and why doing so is beneficial. For example, one school that used these tips for a lesson reported that teenagers in their school were honestly unaware that consuming caffeinated beverages in the afternoon or evening could disrupt their sleep patterns.

Share Strategies to Help Students Manage Anxiety

Many classroom teachers tell us that some students are frequently absent due to anxiety (either ongoing or temporary due to a particular situation). These students stay home to avoid anxious thoughts and feelings about matters such as academic performance, test taking, or peer or adult relationships. They do not know techniques or have not figured out how to regularly implement strategies for managing these feelings and associated symptoms. You can provide parents and students with the tips shown in "Help Your Student Cope with Anxious Thoughts and Feelings: Relaxation and Anxiety Management Strategies" in Appendix B. Review them with your class community during times when increased anxiety is predictable (e.g., before and during high-stakes testing, whenever a significant national or local crisis occurs, or when the school community or a class is experiencing significant upheaval or uncertainty).

Provide Recommendations for Establishing a Consistent Bedtime and Morning Routine

Some students may struggle to get to school because they (and their parents) have difficulty keeping a consistent evening and morning routine. Every day may be a struggle to wake up on time, dress, gather all materials, and get in the car or on the bus on time. This situation leads to a chaotic and stressful start to each day, as well as an increased likelihood of students being tardy or absent. Provide tips to parents on how to establish routines, and consider how teaching all students these routines can help families and students establish healthy life skills. For students whose parents can't or won't participate in getting them ready for school, the handout in Appendix B, "Take the Stress Out of Your Morning Routine: Tips for Establishing Effective Bedtime and Morning Habits" provides essential information for students to self-manage these routine despite family circumstances.

Consider Other Problems that Contribute to Absenteeism with Which Parents Can Assist

It may be beneficial to develop tip sheets and other information on topics such as:

- The importance of attending school on the days prior to and directly after winter and spring vacation
- Late start and early release days are important days for learning, too!
- How to identify, respond to, and report bullying and cyberbullying
- The importance of hand washing and other health tips (especially during cold and flu season)
- Teaching healthy dating and relationship habits
- How to access supports available in the school and broader community for issues such as mental or physical health, addiction services, and homelessness
- How to help students with homework routines and organizational and social skills
- Self-advocacy skills and how to communicate ongoing concerns to the teachers and school

Many reputable sources have information available via the Internet or in free brochures or pamphlets that can help you compile these tip sheets. You might also consult with local health care providers and district personnel to seek out relevant information and resources.

Build Positive Relationships with Parents

One of the other critical factors for working with parents as partners in your classroom attendance initiative is to build and maintain positive relationships with them, and this comes from your communication style and from making frequent overt efforts to provide positive acknowledgments of students. It is easy to fall into the trap of calling on parents only when there is a problem with student behavior, participation, or another serious concern. However, over time, this tends to break down positive relationships between parents and teachers. Some parents may give up because they are not sure how to help, and other parents may become overtly hostile to the teacher or school.

Jessica had numerous students in her middle school classroom for students with behavioral disorders whose parents had never before received a positive communication from the school. She made it her goal to maintain at least a 3:1 ratio of positive to corrective communications with every family member and attributes the turnaround of many of her students to this focus on positive communication. Once parents realized that Jessica saw the good aspects of their children as well, they became active and willing participants and partners in supporting the students in Jessica's classroom environment. She developed the following strategy to help her monitor this ratio.

Use a Color-Coded Phone Call Log

Design a phone call log that can be used to make brief notes about any phone call or other contact (see Figure 5.3 for an example). This log can be used to monitor all communications with parents, including positive and corrective calls, e-mails, and other communication about attendance, behavior, and academics. Use a highlighter or other method to code positive contacts in one color and corrective contacts in another color. Periodically analyze the log to make sure you are maintaining at least a 3:1 ratio of positive to corrective parent contacts for your whole class and for each individual student.

It can be daunting to consider ways to increase these personal contacts with parents because of the constant pressures on your time; however, we have found that positive phone calls, letters, and e-mails take almost no time (usually less than a minute per communication), and the benefits they can bring for building relationships with your parents and students are immense. For a student who has never received a positive phone call home but has received many negative communications, these contacts allow parents to see that you have witnessed and taken active notice of the good in their child. For a student who is simply average or somewhat shy and reserved, these contacts help assure parents that you notice their child and take an active interest. They also tend to leave you feeling good about your day, so we often recommend that you end each day or each week with a few of these positive communications.

Whenever you have to make a corrective contact for any reason, make an intentional effort to follow up with the parents as soon as possible with a few positive communications. Notice that Jonah Getta's corrective call on the sample log was followed up relatively quickly by a positive call and a positive letter home. If the problem gets better, these contacts should acknowledge progress and thank the parents for their role in supporting the student. If the problem doesn't get better, seek out opportunities to provide positive recognition of another area where the student exhibits strength or

FIGURE 5.3 **Sample Phone Call Log**

Name	Date	Time	Reason for Call	Notes
Jackie Alvarez	10/12	1:30	Positive call about helping in class	I reported that Jackie went above and beyond to help an upset peer calm down. Mom thanked me for the call.
Martin Sommers	10/15	3:00	Positive call about overcoming frustration	Called dad and reported that Martin followed prompts to use relaxation strategies when frustrated in math. Dad said they are working to reinforce these strategies at home and thanked me for the call.
Jonah Getta	10/15	3:03	Corrective call about teasing peers	Spoke with mom and dad about the last several days of having to reprimand for inappropriate teasing. They said they would speak with him. Plan to call back tomorrow with an update.
Jonah Getta	10/16	11:15	Positive call about teasing peers problem (better)	Left a message on mom's phone to let her know Jonah was much better this morning. Thanked her for their help with this issue.
Alyssa Black	10/19	3:30	Positive letter home about attendance	Sent home postcard thanking parents and Alyssa for ensuring that she comes to school on time.
Jonah Getta	10/22	3:30	Positive e-mail home about teasing problem (better)	Sent e-mail to mom and dad letting them know that the teasing problem is eliminated. Jonah has had four great days since the phone call.
Jackie Alvarez	10/22	3:35	Corrective call about nonparticipation	Called and let mom know that Jackie has been putting her head down and having difficulty participating the last two days. Communicated concern and asked if mom knew of anything that might be going on. Mom said that a close relative is very ill and Jackie may be worried about that. She said she would speak to her and get back to me. I indicated I would try to show a little extra TLC in the meantime.

growth so that when you have to communicate about the problem, the student's parents know that you are also working to identify positive things about their child.

Maintain Inviting and Supportive Communication

All communications with parents, whether individual or whole class, should seek to maintain a positive, welcoming, and supportive tone. While you will inevitably have to communicate concerns to parents, strive to communicate a rationale for why you have concerns and how changes will help their student be successful, and avoid anything that conveys disappointment or frustration with the student. For example, when communicating with a family about a student's ongoing attendance or tardy concerns, focus on why regular attendance and being on time is critical to the student's success in your class and beyond, rather than expressing the frustration of continually having to catch the student up.

This tone can also be conveyed by directly inviting parents to participate in school and class activities and other aspects of their child's education. Make frequent efforts to remind parents how they can volunteer in the school and your classroom, and find ways for parents who cannot commit to hours of volunteer work to still be involved. For example, one classroom teacher shared with us that she advertised a "dads drop-off" and a "moms drop-off" morning. Any parents who are available come and stand outside her classroom for five minutes before class to greet students as they enter the room. Another teacher told us that she sends home frequent letters inviting parents to come to her high school class for five to 10 minutes sometime during each month at their convenience to view what is going on in the class. With any of these procedures, if necessary, have parents follow district protocols for being in the school and volunteering.

■ ■ ■ ■ ■

Many educators feel helpless when it comes to addressing attendance issues because they view it as primarily a parent problem that they have limited power to change. Our work with schools has shown us that most parents simply have no idea how important regular attendance is for the success of their students and that simple strategies can go a long way to change the behavior of many parents. In this chapter we provided a range of strategies that you can use to increase parents' awareness and ability to ensure that their child is in school every day possible. Strategies in the next chapter address ways to work with parents in the early stages when chronic absenteeism is identified. It also provides recommendations for how to solicit support from other members of the school community and beyond when you identify a more resistant and complex absenteeism problem.

Summary of Chapter 5 Tasks

Communicate about attendance goals and data:

- Identify strategies you will use with parents to generate understanding and enthusiasm for your classroom attendance goals.
- Determine when and how you will regularly update parents about their student's attendance.
- Determine when materials will be developed and how you plan to distribute them on a regular basis.

Provide strategies for addressing common issues that contribute to absenteeism:

- Determine how to increase parent awareness about common problems that contribute to absenteeism, and provide strategies to support parent involvement.
- Determine how to increase communication with families during predictably problematic times of year (e.g., immediately before and after major school breaks, during cold and flu season).

Build positive relationships with parents:

- Identify one or more ways to provide positive acknowledgments to parents about student successes and strengths.
- Identify one or more ways in which you will be directly invitational to parents and provide supportive communication.
- Mark times in your calendar (e.g., approximately every two months) when you will evaluate if you are maintaining a positive ratio of interactions with parents and have made recent efforts to be invitational to parents.

6

Implementing Effective Intervention Plans

Interventions range from wide-ranging plans (Tier 1) to small group or simple individual plans (Tier 2) to highly individualized and more complex plans (Tier 3). Once you have implemented effective prevention procedures at a whole-class (Tier 1) level as discussed in previous chapters, you can begin to identify students with more resistant attendance problems. Some of these students may have shown no improvement with universal procedures, such as lessons and motivational systems. Others may have responded initially—their attendance improved for a short time and then began to decline again. These students require something more to sustain regular attendance patterns.

Relatively simple interventions should be tried first before moving to interventions that require more time and resources. The early-stage classroom interventions described at the beginning of this chapter will be designed and delivered primarily by you. We then provide suggestions for how to enlist additional support from administrators, counselors or social workers, a multidisciplinary team, and in some cases community support for more ongoing and complex absenteeism issues.

Implement Early-Stage Classroom Interventions

As a classroom teacher, you are the primary staff member who interacts with students, and thus, we recommend that you take the lead in the earliest stages of addressing an attendance problem with students and families. The following strategies can make this a less daunting task. They are designed to be minimally time-invasive and still have great potential for positive effects. We have had many teachers tell us that they are surprised when even a student with 60 absences or more has responded to these relatively simple interventions. Sometimes small amounts of additional support are enough to help change attendance patterns.

Initial Phone Calls

Whenever a student has been absent several days in a row or is identified as having a problematic pattern across a month or two, contact families with a phone call to discuss the problem. These calls should be welcoming and supportive. Emphasize that the student is missed when absent and that it is important for the student to be in class every day. Consider using a guided script to preplan what you will say (see Figure 6.1 for an example).

If the student's attendance improves, quickly follow up with parents and provide positive feedback and appreciation to the family for helping the student get to school each day. If you make one or more phone calls and determine that these calls are not making a difference, or the problems indicated by the family are beyond your knowledge or capacity to support, you can try one or more of the other strategies listed in this section, or request additional assistance from a school counselor, psychologist, behavior specialist, or problem-solving team. However, to keep the intervention process as seamless as possible, we recommend that you remain involved in subsequent conversations and interventions as much as possible.

Implement Planned Discussions with Students

Note

The planned discussion described here is adapted from Intervention A in Interventions, *by Randy Sprick and Mickey Garrison (2008) and used with permission.*

A planned discussion is a focused meeting with a student at a time that is free from distractions and interruptions. For students who have not responded to general classroom and schoolwide information about the importance of regular attendance, a private meeting with you may convey the seriousness of the problem and show them that you notice and care when they are absent. To prepare for the meeting:

FIGURE 6.1 **Guided Script for Early-Stage Phone Calls Home**

Hello Mr./Ms.________________________,

This is [insert student's name]'s teacher. How are you today?

I'm calling because I've noticed that [insert student's name] has been absent ____ times in the last month, and I want to make sure that everything is okay and that we are doing everything we can to support [insert student's name] being in school.

We really miss [insert student's name] when [he/she] is gone, and I especially miss [discuss student strengths].

At [insert school name], we are really working to make sure that every student in our school has the best opportunity for success, and we know that this happens when students are in school every day when they are not seriously ill. Our goal is for every student to have fewer than nine absences across the school year because we know this gives our students the best likelihood of success in school and beyond. However, we also know that it can be really difficult for students to be in school every day. We are committed to making sure that we work with each student and each family if there are any things that make it difficult for a child to be in school regularly.

Can you tell me why [insert student's name] has been absent and if there is anything that makes it particularly difficult for [insert student's name] to be in school?

- *If parents are reluctant to discuss the problem*, conclude by indicating that you are pleased when the student is in class and hope that the parents will reach out if there is anything you or the school can do to ensure that the student is present each day. Provide contact information for the school counselor and administrator.
- *If parents mention challenges that you can help problem solve*, spend time discussing ideas with them or schedule a follow-up call or conference at a convenient time. For example, if their child frequently complains about being sick, but they don't know whether staying at home is warranted, guide them in how to use the "How Sick Is Too Sick for School" form (see Appendix B). If the form indicates that the student should probably come to school, assure the parents that they should bring their child to school and let you know about the symptoms the child is reporting. You will carefully monitor the child throughout the day and send the child home if the illness worsens.
- *If parents mention challenges that are beyond your capacity to support*, work to facilitate communication with the school counselor, administrator, or other personnel. Let parents know that you will remain a part of the problem-solving process as much as possible.

- ***Determine when to meet individually with the student.*** This meeting could occur during a well-managed independent work period, when other students are highly engaged in an independent activity, or during lunch or recess. Be careful to schedule the meeting during a time when it will not feel punitive and the student will not be distracted or rushing to get to the next activity. If needed, ask if an interventionist (e.g., the school counselor) can monitor your class for 10 minutes so you can have a private discussion with the student.
- ***Plan to keep a written record of the discussion.*** Before the meeting, print a record of the student's attendance and make note of any specific points that you would like to discuss. For an example, see Figure 6.2.

During the meeting, state your concerns; brainstorm actions that the student, you, or other staff can do to support the student and resolve attendance problems; and set up an informal action plan. Consider the following strategies to guide the discussion:

- *Work to sensitively communicate concerns about attendance and get clarity from the student.* As you discuss the student's attendance record and your concerns, make it clear that you are not attaching blame or accusing the student but rather looking for ways to collectively work together to problem solve. Encourage the student to share his or her perspective about challenges the student is facing in coming to school regularly. If the student is reluctant to discuss the situation or disclose reasons for absences, work together to look at the attendance record and identify patterns. For example, you might look at the reasons on the record for absences and gently probe for more information (e.g., "I see that you were excused for illness three times in October. Do you remember what was going on then?").
- *Brainstorm actions that you and the student can take to resolve attendance concerns.* Work with the student to create a list of ways that the student, teachers, the student's family, the school, or community might help the student be in school regularly. Encourage the student to come up with as many ideas as possible—nothing is silly or out of the range of possibilities when brainstorming. Let the student know that you will both come back to the ideas on the list when you work together to make a plan.

FIGURE 6.2 **Planned Discussion Record**

Student ______________________ Teacher ______________________ Date ________

Describe the problem: Number of absences ______ Absence category ____________

Describe specific of reasons for absences and anything else discussed as part of the problem:

____

____

____

____

____

____

Brainstorm (*What can you do? What can I do? What can others do?*):

____

____

____

____

____

____

____

Select actions and identify who will be responsible for doing each action:

____

____

____

____

____

____

____

Set up next meeting date and time: ________

A relevant example of this step involves a student we worked with who was having problems with peers on the bus, a situation that was causing him to avoid school. We worked with him to brainstorm a list of possible actions we could all take to solve the problem. Some of the possibilities included an assigned seat for him or the other students, identifying a bus buddy (an older peer to sit with), and looking for carpools or walking or school bus options. These possibilities ranged from relatively simple solutions, such as the assigned seat, to things like the walking or school bus, which would require at least two adult volunteers and far more coordination and effort.

- *Set up an informal action plan.* Work with the student to pick a few actions on the brainstormed list that are manageable and likely to help. When possible, keep the plan relatively simple at this stage of intervention, and identify strategies that do not require a huge amount of involvement or change from other people, such as the student's parents or interventionists in the school. Strategies that help the student focus on the goal of regular attendance and demonstrate your commitment and support are especially beneficial. If additional efforts and personnel are warranted, work with the student to identify simple preliminary strategies that you can both start right away. Schedule a subsequent meeting with the student and other people identified as part of the plan.

For the student in the school bus example, we discovered that he had a phone with music on it that he carried each day, but he had no headphones. He thought that if he could just listen to music and tune out the other students, the problem might go away. We let him borrow a pair of headphones to keep in his backpack, and we recommended that he sit near the bus driver, as the other students liked to sit at the back of the bus. Using these simple strategies helped reduce his anxiety about being on the bus, and he found that when he ignored the other students, they began to ignore him as well. He finished the remainder of the year on the bus without problems, and his attendance improved.

- *Schedule a follow-up meeting.* Schedule a follow-up meeting within two weeks of the initial discussion. Knowing that there will be a sustained effort to resolve the problem brings an increased sense of accountability and likelihood of action for you and the student. It also ensures that the student will be recognized for improvements and that the plan will be revised if needed. If the student continues to struggle with attendance, consider implementing other ideas that were brainstormed, and bring in additional problem-solving processes, personnel, and interventions as appropriate.

Work with the Student to Self-Monitor Attendance

To help the student remain focused on the goal of improved attendance, have the student fill out an Attendance Monitoring form (see Figure 6.3) each day. Have the student initial or color in the box for each day of attendance. At the end of the week, have the student tally up the number of absences accrued during the week, and at the end of the month, have the student add up the number of absences accrued during the month. Also have the student add the current month's absences to the number of absences in prior months to determine the total absences to date. You can then work with the student to determine an attendance category for the month (regular, at-risk, chronic), as well as for the year to date.

If you are also concerned about partial-day absences (e.g., tardies or early departure from class or school), have the student color-code the chart in different colors for full days of attendance as compared with partial days. You might also have the student write the number of minutes of school missed for each tardy or early departure and monitor the number of minutes of class missed throughout the week and month.

Individualized Motivational Systems

For some students, a motivational system may be appropriate to help the student get a boost in motivation to come to school. However, when using a motivational system, first ensure that the student is able to come to school and that something like a transportation barrier or chronic illness is not preventing the student's attendance. When possible, work with the student to figure out ways to overcome these barriers (e.g., considering a carpool buddy when transportation is a concern). Once you know that it is possible for the student to attend school, you can use an individualized motivational system to increase the likelihood that the student will make choices that enable him to attend.

First, determine if the motivational system will simply track and reinforce improved attendance, or if part of the system will track and reinforce other behaviors that are related to the student's attendance. For example, Jordy was one of Jessica's students who often avoided school because of a

FIGURE 6.3 **Attendance Monitoring Form**

Name: ____

My total number of absences last school year (20___/ 20___) were _____.

Current school year: 20___/ 20___. My goal is no more than _____ absences this school year.

Directions: Fill in the weekday calendar template with the dates that correspond with the current month. Pick a color for each attendance category and color in the days of the month using your coding.

Attendance category:

☐ I was in school all day ☐ I was tardy ☐ I left early ☐ I was absent all day

Month: ______________ Year __________

Monday	Tuesday	Wednesday	Thursday	Friday	Absences each week

Absences this month: ______________ Total absences to date: ___________

significant reading deficit. When he did attend, his behavior would escalate when presented with reading tasks, so Jessica placed him on a reinforcement system that rewarded him for being on task.

Use the General Principles for Reinforcement Systems in Chapter 3 to guide the development of an individualized motivational system. For example, set a reasonable yet challenging goal that is specific to the student. If the student has been absent two days a week on average, set an initial goal of one day of absence or fewer a week. You can also modify some of the Whole-Class Reinforcement Systems in Chapter 3 for use with an individual student. For example, instead of a classroom group contingency, use the same procedures with an individual student, and work with the student to identify rewards she would be personally be interested in (see Appendix A for individualized reinforcement ideas). The Attendance Squares example (in Chapter 3) that is similar to tic-tac-toe and bingo could be modified for an individual student. Have the student draw a token whenever in attendance, and the student earns a Mystery Motivator reward or chance to spin the reward spinner whenever a row is filled—horizontally, vertically, or diagonally.

Implement Simple Function-Based Interventions

With ongoing absenteeism problems, it is important to use a function-based, or cause-based, approach. With this approach, we recognize that any behavior that occurs repeatedly serves a function or has a cause. The goal is to identify what causes or group of causes is maintaining the behavior—in this case, absenteeism. These causes can differ vastly from student to student. One student may have a chronic illness, another may lack adequate supports at home, and another may be seeking to avoid frustration with academic deficits. For many students, multiple contributing factors work together to prevent regular attendance.

Once the cause or causes of the behavior are identified, interventions can be put in place to address that particular function (or functions), thus increasing the likelihood that the intervention will be successful. While other school personnel are typically trained to be the experts in functional behavior assessment—an evidence-based process for determining why a student engages in a particular behavior—we believe it is essential for all staff to have a basic understanding of how to incorporate function into any intervention plan. Consider the following causes of absenteeism that may need to be considered when creating a plan for intervening with chronic absence. While some of these causes may seem outside the realm of what you can influence as a classroom teacher, for each cause there are things that teachers and schools can do that have been demonstrated to make a positive difference in getting students to attend regularly. This chapter concludes with examples of simple function-based intervention strategies that you can implement as a classroom teacher. It also covers how to enlist team support for function-based intervention plans that are outside the scope of what you can implement alone.

Common Causes of Absenteeism

Causes of absenteeism can be broken down in many different ways. For the purposes of this book, we define five broad categories:

- Lack of understanding about the importance of attendance
- Barriers to attendance
- Escape or avoidance
- Desire to obtain or access something outside of school
- Lack of value placed on education

In the following sections, we describe each cause in more detail and provide specific examples.

Lack of Understanding About the Importance of Attendance

Lack of understanding is perhaps the simplest cause to address, especially when a pattern of absenteeism is in the early stages (e.g., the student has just started formal school, or the student has just begun showing increased levels of absenteeism). This cause of absenteeism has two main subsets:

- Parents or students don't recognize the negative effects of absenteeism.
- The school does not place overt value on or emphasize the importance of attendance.

The strategies outlined in Chapters 1 through 5 will go a long way toward addressing this cause.

Barriers to Attendance

Barriers are situations that prevent students from attending school. Even if students value school and want to attend, they encounter difficulties that make it a struggle or even impossible. Examples of common barriers include illness, dental problems, mental health issues such as depression or anxiety, transportation problems, financial issues, and obligations other than school (e.g., a job, watching younger siblings or elderly family members, or caring for a parent with a substance-abuse or mental health issue).

Escape or Avoidance

Many students who are absent may choose to stay out of school or complain of illness so that they can escape or avoid something in the school environment that they find aversive. Students may avoid school because of academic, social, or coping skills deficits that make school a difficult or even threatening environment. We cannot emphasize enough the potency of academic deficits for causing a student to avoid school. These deficits can include an inability to read at grade level, gaps in mathematical knowledge, and difficulties with organizational skills. Because reading permeates all academic subjects and is the gateway for learning most skills in school, we encourage you to give special consideration to how reading difficulties may cause students to avoid school. Consider the potential stress and frustration students with deficits in reading feel when they are continually given academic tasks that are beyond their capability. Academic deficits should also be given careful consideration, as the longer a student exhibits patterns of excessive absence from school, the more likely the student is to suffer academic deficits.

Students may also stay away from school to avoid uncomfortable interactions with people, including conflict with peers or staff members and bullying situations, or because of concerns in the classroom or school climate. When any of the following conditions exist in the school environment, students may be less motivated to attend school or actively try to avoid school:

- Highly punitive and adversarial interactions are occurring between staff and students (e.g., staff members are frequently using sarcasm or belittling students, students perceive that staff members are unfair or disproportionate in their attention to negative behavior). Classrooms or common areas are unsafe or chaotic.
- Students are frequently bored in class and lack engagement in relevant educational activities.
- Students experience embarrassment due to poorly designed or managed activities.
- The overall climate of the school is cold and uninviting.

Desire to Obtain or Access Something Outside of School

Students may find something outside the school environment more satisfying than being in school. They may seek peer or adult attention or access to tangible items and activities that are unavailable in school; they may find joy in school-sponsored or extracurricular activities that take them out of school (sports teams or clubs); or they may want to participate in seasonal activities, such as hunting, fishing, or surfing.

Lack of Value Placed on Education

Student attendance may be affected when a particular parent, culture, or community does not see school as valuable. Absences may also occur when the school or community unintentionally sends messages that school is not "for" particular students or when a systemic societal message indicates that school does not serve certain students. This cause of absenteeism can be particularly difficult to address, but it is a common problem and will need to be addressed in a comprehensive and longitudinal way.

For example, one of Jessica's students came from a family who had a negative and adversarial relationship with the school, and they frequently expressed disgust with the school system in general. This student's parents had both dropped out of high school because of poor experiences, and he had two older brothers who had dropped out of high school. Whenever the student struggled, he would fall back on statements he heard from his family about school being for some kids and not for others and about the system being rigged against him. Working with this student involved significant time and attention to listening to his concerns and the concerns of his family and trying to understand the barriers and struggles they faced in the past with the school system. When they realized that Jessica and her team wanted to listen, understand, and work with the family to find ways to make the school experience work for this student, the student and his parents became far more engaged and willing participants in his schooling.

Simple, Function-Based Interventions

If you identify the cause of a student's absenteeism, consider whether there are relatively simple supports that you can help the student with or strategies that you can implement in the classroom to address that function. The following examples are real stories of teachers who have intervened with students to address particular causes of absenteeism.

Supports to Prevent Asthma Attacks

A teacher saw that a student in her class was frequently absent due to asthma. The teacher worked with her school to get an air purifier in the classroom, and she monitored air pollution and pollen levels each day so that the student would have alternate recess options on days when the air quality was poor. She also sent memos home with all students indicating that they would need to avoid using smelly sprays and lotions, as these are a trigger for respiratory problems. Among other measures, she also ensured that she worked with the family and the district nurse to identify a safety plan for the student so that the student's parents knew the school, and more specifically the teacher, was prepared in case of an emergency. With these measures in place, the student's attendance improved.

Addressing Financial Concerns

One of Jessica's students began avoiding school after becoming homeless and couch surfing or living out of her parents' van. While the student was still highly motivated to attend school, she was embarrassed about her lack of clean clothes. When she had no access to laundry services, she would avoid school until the next time she could wash her clothes. As soon as this pattern was identified, Jessica worked with the student to figure out a schedule when she could discreetly come to the school and use the washer and dryer in the Family and Consumer Studies classroom. With this support, and by connecting her with other supports in the district for homeless youth, the student soon returned to a pattern of regular attendance and academic success.

Troubleshooting Transportation Difficulties

A teacher identified that one of his students frequently missed school because his parents worked early in the morning and could not wake him up for school. He would sleep through his alarm and miss the bus. The teacher worked with the school to get the student an extra alarm clock so that he could set one alarm near him to wake him up and one alarm across the room so that he would have to get out of bed to turn it off. The teacher then put the student on a reinforcement system where he earned points toward a desired item or activity for each day that he attended school. With these simple supports, the student began regularly attending school.

The Simple Act of Noticing

One phenomenal educator shared the following story with us: "There was a 7th grader who was never a problem, and then this year he 'snapped.' He would use words and phrases that he knew would get a reaction and get him out of school. We had conversations with parents and mental health experts, and no one could understand what was going on. After a semester of chasing our tail, I again had a conversation with him. This was not the first conversation I had with him, but it was the first conversation where I asked the RIGHT questions. Long story short, his mom was pregnant, and he was not getting the attention from home that he was used to. I told him, jokingly, that I wished I could give him a hug every time I saw him in the hallway, but I understood that getting a hug from the 33-year-old school resource officer wasn't cool. He looked at me with tears in his eyes and said that he couldn't remember the last time he was hugged. From that moment forward, every time I saw him (three to four times a day), he got a hug. I am in no way saying that solved the problem, but he has not missed a day nor been sent home from school since!"

Enlist Team Support for Resistant Absenteeism Problems

For students who do not respond to universal prevention and early-stage interventions, continued absenteeism is a symptom of problems that are more resistant to change. These problems often require additional supports, so seek out ways to connect with other resources and supports within your school and in the community. Determine whether your school has a student-support team or multidisciplinary team process that you can meet with to access Tier 2 and Tier 3 supports within your school. We define Tier 2 procedures as targeted interventions for students who have not responded to Tier 1 that can be implemented quickly (within three to five days) once a need is identified. These include small-group interventions, such as pullout social skills groups or academic instruction interventions; daily progress report interventions, such as check-in/check-out (CICO) or Connections; and mentoring. Tier 2 interventions also include relatively simple individualized interventions that address a particular cause of absenteeism, such as helping a student who has no access to laundry facilities determine places and times within the school or district where she can wash clothes. Tier 3 supports typically involve functional behavioral assessment, leading to highly individualized intervention plans. For students who require Tier 3 support, use a multidisciplinary team process for assessing the nature of the absenteeism problem and implementing a comprehensive intervention plan. Descriptions of Tier 2 and Tier 3 procedures and examples are available in the companion resource to this book—*School Leader's Guide to Tackling Attendance Challenges*.

If your school does not have a student-support team or multidisciplinary team that you can access, or there is a backlog of students and the team will not be able to help you problem solve in a reasonable amount of time, connect with one or more of your school or district counselors, school psychologists, behavior specialists, social workers, master teachers, or administrative personnel. As you work to address the student's absenteeism concerns, continue to actively work to build a collaborative relationship with parents (see the strategies in Chapter 5). Also consider whether to consult with outside agents (e.g., mental or physical health providers, department of human services personnel, rehabilitation services staff) for assistance in designing or implementing an intervention plan, or both.

We have had lots of educators share their success stories with attendance at all three tiers with us. These examples range from the student who had 60 days of absence the previous year and only five absences once the school initiated a schoolwide awareness campaign (Tier 1), to the student who was given a job to raise the flag each day in the school and began attending regularly so he could meet the responsibilities of his job (Tier 2), to the student who everyone thought was going to drop out but ended up graduating after his school initiated an intensive process of assessment and intervention to address causes of absenteeism (Tier 3). The common component in each of these examples was a relentless commitment from the school to help every student reach the goal of regular attendance. Some of these success stories were much simpler to solve than the educators would have predicted, and some involved intensive time, resources, and supports. However, in all cases, the educators expressed their excitement that the students now had the opportunity for greater success in school because of their improved attendance.

Summary of Chapter 6 Tasks

Implement early-stage interventions:

- Identify students with attendance concerns early in the school year and provide one or more early-stage interventions, such as initial phone calls, planned discussion, self-monitoring, and individualized reinforcement systems.
- Incorporate function-based thinking into intervention plan design.

Enlist team support for ongoing attendance concerns:

- Connect with one or more school personnel or access your school's student support problem-solving team when attendance concerns are not resolved through universal procedures and early-stage interventions.
- Work with a team to design and implement a behavior intervention plan.

Conclusion

In the past, we often failed to address attendance issues in a comprehensive and systematic way. Many educators believed that there was little that could be done to address this issue because it stemmed mainly from parents. They may have felt that changing parent behavior was out of their reach, or that parents who failed to bring their children to school regularly just didn't care much about education. In other cases, absenteeism was viewed as a lesser concern in comparison with academic deficits and behavioral disruptions. When something was done to address absenteeism problems, the approaches were primarily punitive and had limited effects for many students.

This book advocates a shift in both mindset and strategies to address absenteeism. First, increasing student attendance is a goal that is absolutely within reach for our schools and classrooms. In our work supporting schools and individual teachers as they build a culture of attendance, we have seen that attendance is a highly malleable concern that educators have great power to influence. Teachers often express surprise that the relatively simple strategies we describe in this book can make such a huge difference in improving student attendance, across whole classes as well as with individuals. In reality, most students and parents will do the right thing when they are educated about our attendance priorities and provided with useful strategies that empower them to meet expectations. When we educate them about how critical it is for students to attend regularly, attendance improves. When we provide meaningful tools and supports that help students and parents overcome the obstacles that prevent coming to school, and when we actively work to motivate students to attend every day they possibly can, attendance improves.

We also advocate moving away from solely punitive and reactive approaches to absenteeism. Purely punitive approaches are not effective in changing behavior or improving academics. Likewise, waiting for a severe problem to emerge and then attempting to intervene is rarely effective and typically wastes valuable resources, because severe problems require intensive intervention. Instead, we look to apply approaches that are positive and proactive and intervene at the earliest stages of a problem. With this approach, we recommend trying the easiest and cheapest interventions first so that we can match the intensity of the services provided in our classes and schools to the intensity of each student's need for support. By implementing good universal practices at a classroom level and staging early interventions at the first signs of a problem, we can reduce the number of students who require time and resource-intensive interventions that occur outside of the classroom.

We strongly believe that attendance is a critical variable that schools must address. Although, as a classroom teacher, you have an unbelievable number of priorities to tackle, attendance is essential for student success, and if students are not in school, no other priority, initiative, or strategy can realize its full potential. As educators, we simply cannot ignore patterns of absenteeism. For students to be successful in school, they first have to be *in* school. For academic and behavioral initiatives to be successful, students have to be present enough to benefit from those efforts. We hope that the strategies and resources in this book have motivated you to tackle absenteeism and given you the tools you need to build and support a classroom culture of attendance.

Appendix A
Student Reinforcers

The following are ideas for classroom and individual student incentives that can be selected for intermittent rewards or used within a structured reinforcement system. This list is not exhaustive, and you can get creative with options for reinforcement. Work with your students to identify rewards that would be motivating for them.

Classroom

- Class game (e.g., Heads-Up Seven-Up, team competition with group video game, charades)
- Certificates of recognition (whole class, individual student) awarded by the principal, you, or another valued staff member
- Special day (e.g., hat day, funky apparel day, crazy sock day)
- Letters or postcards mailed home to congratulate the class on achievement
- Extra recess or extended recess time
- Read aloud a book of students' choice
- Class party (e.g., confetti party, ice cream party, disco dance party, flashlight reading party with lights out)

- Quick goofy activity (e.g., make armpit noises for 30 seconds, have a snowball fight with recycled paper for 20 seconds)
- Free time (e.g., chat break at end of class, choice of activities for *x* minutes)
- Choose study buddies or where to sit for the day
- Nature walk or in-school scavenger hunt (i.e., include a list of items students must find on a walk)
- Field trip
- Class time in supervised computer lab, library, gym, or another classroom
- Permission to use cell phone, tablet, computer, or personal music device (with headphones) in class

Individual

- Recognition mailed home or positive phone call home (teacher or principal)
- Choice of seat for the day (e.g., teacher's chair or next to a friend)
- Have lunch with someone (e.g., lunch with the principal or teacher, lunch in a special location in school with two friends)
- Art/school supplies or gift certificate to school store
- Small item (e.g., hand stamp, sticker, temporary tattoo, Silly Putty, pencils/erasers, bubbles, action figures, sports or game trading cards, sunglasses, hair ornaments, comic books, or Mad Libs party game)
- Be a helper for someone (principal, custodian, librarian, specialist)
- Decorate a ceiling tile, wall, or sidewalk
- Help prepare an activity (e.g., plan assembly, teach lesson, create YouTube video)
- Discount or free admission to activity (e.g., rock-climbing wall, ice rink, aquarium, sporting event, movie)
- Record a message for school's or teacher's answering machine or video for the school website
- First choice of activity or first in line (e.g., lunch line, lab activity)
- Play a game or do a preferred activity for *x* amount of time

Appendix B
Handouts for Families

You may find it helpful to provide any or all of the following handouts to families as a means of having them work with you toward improving student attendance:

- Handout for Families on Dealing with Technology—Dealing with Technology: Tips and Strategies for Families
- Handout for Families on Deciding When a Child Should Stay Home—How Sick Is Too Sick for School?
- Handout for Families on Sleep Habits—Tips for Improving Your Child's Sleep and Reducing Absenteeism
- Handout for Families on Anxiety—Help Your Student Cope with Anxious Thoughts and Feelings: Relaxation and Anxiety Management Strategies
- Handout for Families on Establishing Bedtime and Morning Routines—Take the Stress Out of Your Morning Routine: Tips for Establishing Effective Bedtime and Morning Habits

Handout for Families on Dealing with Technology—Dealing with Technology: Tips and Strategies for Families

In today's world, technology is everywhere. Children are exposed to technology in a multitude of forms throughout each day. They text, e-mail, use social media, surf the web, watch TV and movies—the list goes on and on. In fact, for many children, technology is one of the main ways they interact with and learn about the world. Thus, it is important that they have some guidance as they negotiate this increasingly technological world.

This tip sheet can help you consider what you can do to help your children remain safe, act responsibly with technology, and learn how to be good digital citizens. If you have any questions, please contact me at 555-1234.

Talk Early and Often with Your Children About Safety When Dealing with Technology

Inform children that:

- They should never share passwords with anyone other than parents or guardians (not even with a best friend).
- They should never give out personally identifiable information.
- They should never give anyone their location or agree to meet in person with anyone they met online.

Discuss Identity Theft, Sexual and Financial Predators, and Other Risks

Frequently discuss (in age-appropriate terms) and review what appropriate and respectful behavior looks and sounds like when communicating through technology. Use the following guidelines:

- If you wouldn't do or say something in front of a trusted and respected adult, don't do it online or by text.
- Participating in cyberbullying by sharing, reposting, or commenting on negative remarks about someone else makes the problem worse. The only appropriate response is to not respond and tell a parent or another adult about the cyberbullying immediately.
- If you wouldn't want a comment shared or said about you, don't share or say it about another person.

- Think before you post or text, especially if you are upset or angry. Once a photo or message is in the electronic world, it never really goes away and can seriously affect your reputation, success, and future.
- NEVER send photos or images that contain nudity or messages with sexually explicit content. (*Note:* Sexting—sending sexually explicit photos or messages by phone or other technology—is a phenomenon that has become increasingly common, especially among teenage girls. It carries serious risks, such as messages being forwarded to others. In addition, those who send or possess sexually explicit photos of a minor can face felony child pornography charges.)

Establish Procedures and Rules Regarding Technology in Your Household

Set appropriate limits on how long and where technology can be used. Consider procedures and rules, such as the following:

- Allow no more than two hours of nonacademic technology each day on weekends, and less on weekdays.
- Some cell phones and computers can be set to have time limits or to prevent access during specified hours. Create a password for your child and set the device with the desired restrictions.
- Require that all electronic devices be turned off one hour before the child's bedtime. Studies have shown that bright lights (such as those from computers, cell phones, and TVs) can interrupt human sleep cycles and delay sleep.
- During meals, place all cell phones (including parents' phones!) in a box away from the table.
- Create the expectation that electronic devices are not allowed in children's bedrooms. This includes cell phones, computers, TVs, and gaming devices. One possible way to set this expectation is to establish a charging station in the parents' bedroom; all charging cords stay at this station. At bedtime, place all electronic devices in the parents' room to charge. Technology should not be allowed in children's bedrooms for several reasons:
  - Electronic devices in bedrooms have been linked to sleep problems in children and teens. Lack of sleep contributes to attention problems, difficulty concentrating and learning, aggressive

behavior, increased risk of depression, and a host of other health, behavioral, and emotional issues.

  - Access to technology in the privacy of the bedroom can lead to increased risk for sexting, cyberbullying, conflict, and engaging in behaviors that can put a child at risk for predatory behavior.
  - For children who have unsupervised access to technology, night is a prime time for cyberbullying. When children are victimized through cyberbullying, it is important to limit and monitor their access to technology so that they are not bombarded with negative messages 24 hours a day.

- Create a technology contract that outlines specific rules and expectations for your children's use of technology. Include expectations for time, location, respectful and appropriate behavior, responsible use of personal information, appropriate and inappropriate sites, and how use will be monitored and supervised. You may wish to include "responsibility clauses" that allow children additional technology privileges for exceptional behavior, as well as penalty clauses that outline potential consequences for violating aspects of the contract.

Supervise and Teach Your Child About Technology Use

Although filters and parental control features are available and can be a useful starting place, be aware that many children know how to bypass these controls. In addition, your child will likely visit places with no filters and no supervision. Therefore, the best supervisor and teacher is YOU!

Talk with your children about the websites they visit, what they do there, and who they communicate with.

When your children are first exploring technology, explore it with them and give guidance about good versus bad sites, how to evaluate the information they are viewing, and how to make responsible and safe decisions.

Periodically review your children's cell phone and computer histories. Set the expectation that only a designated adult can erase cell phone, browser, and e-mail histories. If the child erases the history, the adult should assume that something inappropriate has occurred and put consequences in place.

Over time, as your children demonstrate increased maturity, responsibility, and appropriate use of technology, you may decide to gradually release responsibility to them. However, always remain involved by talking with your children, providing periodic spot checks, and reminding them about the essentials of safety and responsibility as digital citizens.

Additional Resources

- Common Sense Media: commonsensemedia.org
- Family Online Safety Institute: www.fosi.org
- "Internet Safety Tips for Parents," U.S. Department of Justice: www.justice.gov/usao/ian/psc/Elementary%20Safety%20Tips%20for%20Parents.pdf
- Tip sheets on a variety of topics, National Center for Missing and Exploited Children: https://www.netsmartz.org/TipSheets
- "10 Ways to Keep Kids Safe Online," Tech Savvy: techsavvymag.com/2014/04/07/online-safety-kids-parents/
- "Tips for Parents," National Crime Prevention Council: http://archive.ncpc.org/topics/internet-safety/tips-for-parents.html

Source: From *Foundations Module E: Improving Safety, Managing Conflict, and Reducing Bullying,* by R. Sprick, J. Sprick, and P. Rich, 2014, Eugene, OR: Ancora Publishing. Copyright 2014 by Ancora Publishing. Adapted with permission.

Handout for Families on Deciding When a Child Should Stay Home—How Sick Is Too Sick for School?

In general, children are too sick to come to school when either:

- They are contagious.
- Their symptoms are serious enough to prevent them from focusing on the tasks they need to do in school.

Use this checklist to determine whether to keep your child home from school.

	YES	NO
1. Does your child have a fever of 100°F or higher?	___	___
2. Has your child vomited two or more times in a 24-hour period?	___	___
3. Does your child have diarrhea?	___	___
4. Are your child's eyes crusty, bright red, or discharging yellow or green fluid (conjunctivitis/pink eye)?	___	___
5. If your child complains of a sore throat, is it accompanied by fever, headache, stomachache, or swollen glands?	___	___
6. If your child complains of a stomachache, is it accompanied by fever, vomiting, diarrhea, lethargy, sharp pain, or a hard belly?	___	___
7. Does your child have a persistent, phlegmy cough?	___	___
8. Does your child have lice (white, translucent eggs the size of a pinpoint on the hair or insects on the scalp)?	___	___

If you answered yes to any of these questions, please keep your child home from school and consider seeking medical attention. Your child could have a serious or contagious illness. Keep your child home until symptom-free for at least 24 hours or until the doctor indicates that the child can return to school.

Children who have a cold, headache, or stomachache that is not accompanied by fever, vomiting, or diarrhea can probably come to school.

If your child has a rash, it could be contagious. Please seek medical advice before allowing your child to come to school.

Earaches are not contagious. Children can come to school if they can concentrate on their work.

Once your child has been treated for lice, he can return to school.

Source: From *Absenteeism and Truancy: Interventions and Universal Procedures,* by W. R. Jenson, R. Sprick, J. Sprick, H. Majszak, and L. Phosaly, 2014, Eugene, OR: Ancora Publishing. Copyright 2014 by Ancora Publishing. Adapted with permission.

Handout for Families on Sleep Habits—Tips for Improving Your Child's Sleep and Reducing Absenteeism

Did you know that your child (6 to 13 years old) needs 9 to 11 hours of sleep a night? Did you know that your teenager (14 to 17 years old) needs 8 to 10 hours of sleep a night? Inadequate sleep can lead to the following:

- Mood swings
- Behavioral problems
- Exacerbated symptoms of ADHD or misdiagnosis of ADHD
- Problems with learning
- Illness

Here are some tips to help your child get adequate sleep:

- Minimize activities that involve bright lights, excitement, or stress in the hour before bedtime, including the following:
    - Exercise
    - Playing video games
    - Using cell phones
    - Watching TV (as watching TV near bedtime has been associated with bedtime resistance, difficulty falling asleep, anxiety around sleep, and sleeping fewer hours)
- Restrict cell phones and other electronic devices from your child's bedroom during sleeping hours. For example, have a charging station in your room where all electronic devices charge at night. (This is important for sleep, as well as for reducing cyberbullying and other concerns that can come with unsupervised technology use.)
- Keep a regular and consistent sleep schedule and bedtime routine, even on weekends.
- Make your child's bedroom conducive to sleep—dark, cool, and quiet.
- Have your child avoid caffeine throughout the day and especially after midday.
- Have your child avoid large meals before bedtime.

Source: Based on information from the National Sleep Foundation and Centers for Disease Control and Prevention.

Handout for Families on Anxiety—Help Your Student Cope with Anxious Thoughts and Feelings: Relaxation and Anxiety Management Strategies

Most people experience anxiety or stress at one time or another. However, high levels of anxiety or stress can have negative effects, such as increased absenteeism, physical illness, and struggles in school. The following tips can help your child manage anxiety and cope with stressful situations (noting that if your child has significant and ongoing struggles with anxious thoughts and feelings, you should consider discussing this situation with your doctor, the school counselor, or another health professional to determine if additional supports are warranted):

1. Work with your child to identify and record times and places that trigger anxious feelings. Also identify physiological changes that result from anxiety. Have the child reflect on times when anxious and identify if any of the following occurred: sweating, feeling shaky, increased heartbeat, or tension in certain parts of the body. If your child is unable to identify anxiety triggers or symptoms, it may be helpful for him to write in a journal whenever anxious feelings occur. Work together to look for a pattern across time.
2. Teach and practice relaxation techniques with your child. Model and talk aloud as you initially demonstrate a technique. Then have your child practice with you. As your child demonstrates the ability to perform the technique with ease, encourage thinking about an anxiety-producing situation while practicing the technique. Encourage your child to use one or more of the following relaxation techniques when in anxiety-producing situations and when experiencing identified physiological symptoms. Find time each evening to practice one or more techniques together:
   - *Deep Breathing.* Have your child sit with a straight back or lie down and breathe normally and notice how a normal breath feels. Demonstrate and then have your child practice breathing deeply, inhaling through the nose. The abdomen should expand as she breathes deeply and fills the lungs. The chest and shoulders should move only minimally. To exhale, your child should breathe slowly out through the mouth using an audible exhaling sound. Practice the technique while counting: four seconds to inhale, seven seconds holding the breath, eight seconds exhaling. Do at least 10

full-breath sequences during practice each day, and encourage additional sequences whenever your child is feeling anxious.

- *Progressive Muscle Relaxation.* Have your child tense his toes (tightening the muscles as much as possible), hold for at least five seconds, and then release. Have your child tense his calf muscles, tightening the muscles as much as possible, and then release. Have your child work progressively through each major muscle group (i.e., thighs, buttocks, abdomen, arms and hands, neck and shoulders, jaw and lips, eyes). Direct your child to feel the difference between tension and relaxation. Discuss which muscles could be tensed and relaxed when feeling anxious in the presence of others. The student could tense his toes, leg muscles, or hands without others knowing he is using the technique.
- *Visualization.* Have your child identify a place or situation that is calming and ask him or her to describe as much as possible about the situation—sights, sounds, smells, and physical sensations (e.g., heat, texture of the ground). Have your child sit and close his or her eyes. Initially practice by describing the place as your child visualizes being in that place. Over time, switch to having your child visualize without any auditory cues.

3. Work with your child to maintain other healthy lifestyle choices that can help your child feel best:
   - Drink plenty of water and limit caffeine.
   - Get recommended amounts of exercise.
   - Get adequate sleep for age group. Children ages 6 through 13 need approximately 9 to 11 hours of sleep a night, and teenagers ages 14 through 17 need 8 to 10 hours of sleep each night.
   - Do healthy things that your child enjoys and finds relaxing. Consider things like yoga, listening to music, volunteering, or talking to friends or family who have a positive and optimistic outlook and lifestyle.
   - Get help for depression or anxiety as needed. Talk to someone at school or discuss ongoing concerns with a physician or therapist.

Other Resources

- Anxiety and Depression Association of America, "Tips to Manage Anxiety and Stress" (adaa.org/tips-manage-anxiety-and-stress)
- Harvard Health Publishing, "Relaxation Techniques: Breath Control Helps Quell Errant Stress Response" (https://www.health.harvard.edu/mind-and-mood/relaxation-techniques-breath-control-helps-quell-errant-stress-response)
- Mayo Clinic, "Relaxation Techniques: Try These Steps to Reduce Stress" (www.mayoclinic.org/healthylifestyle/stress-management/in-depth/relaxation-technique/art-20045368)

Source: From *Bullying Solutions: Universal and Individual Strategies* (p. 582), by J. Sprick, W. R. Jenson, R. Sprick, and C. Coughlin, 2017, Eugene, OR: Ancora Publishing. Copyright 2017 by Ancora Publishing. Adapted with permission.

Handout for Families on Establishing Bedtime and Morning Routines—Take the Stress Out of Your Morning Routine: Tips for Establishing Effective Bedtime and Morning Habits

An hour before the bus will arrive, your child's alarm goes off. She hits the snooze button. The alarm goes off again. Snooze. You come in and tell your child to get out of bed. Ten minutes later, she is still not up. You throw the covers off and tell her to hop in the shower. After she showers, she takes 10 minutes to figure out what to wear. When she saunters down the stairs, she has 15 minutes left to eat breakfast and get her things together. She turns on the TV and slowly eats her breakfast. With three minutes before the bus arrives, she runs around throwing things into her bag. As she runs out the door, you realize that she has left one of her books behind. You run out the door after her.

If this scene or something similar plays out in your household, consider ways to establish consistent nighttime and morning routines. Have your child start getting ready for bed at least 30 minutes before the specified bedtime so that she gets everything ready for the next day and starts winding down for bed. Use a checklist like the one shown here before your child goes to bed each night so that you and your child won't need to scramble in the morning to get everything ready. After the routine is established, you may find that getting everything organized for the morning will also allow your student to sleep in a little later.

Before Bedtime

Tasks	Completed
1. Pack school bag.	☐
Homework? ☐ yes ☐ no	
Binder? ☐ yes ☐ no	
Pencil? ☐ yes ☐ no	
2. Pack lunch and put in fridge.	☐
3. Set out clothes.	☐
4. Set alarm.	☐
5. Brush teeth.	☐

Teach your child that the snooze button is not helpful, and consider taping over it or buying an alarm clock without a snooze function. Use a morning checklist to set a routine and ensure that your child reaches school with all of the necessities.

In the Morning

Tasks	Completed
1. Get up with alarm. (No snooze!)	☐
2. Shower (10 minutes max) and get dressed.	☐
3. Brush teeth.	☐
4. Put lunch in bag.	☐
5. Take bag and wait for bus.	☐

You may also wish to provide a reinforcing item or activity for your child when he uses the checklist and gets to school or the bus on time. For example, "After you use your bedtime and morning checklist and get to school on time for 10 days, I will take you and a friend to a basketball game." If a particular part of the routine is difficult for your child, consider reinforcing only that part. For example, if your child habitually hits snooze and you have to nag to get him or her up, reinforce when your child does not use the snooze button. For example, "After five days of getting up without snooze or nagging, you get 30 minutes of extra TV time in the evening."

Bibliography

Alexander, K. L., Entwisle, D. R., & Horsey, C. S. (1997). From first grade forward: Early foundations of high school dropout. *Sociology of Education, 70*(2), 87–107.

Archer, A. L., & Hughes, C. A. (2011). *Explicit instruction: Effective and efficient teaching.* New York: Guilford Press.

Attendance Works and Everyone Graduates Center. (2017). *Portraits of change: Aligning school and community resources to reduce chronic absence.* Retrieved from https://www.attendanceworks.org/portraits-of-change/

Balfanz, R., & Byrnes, V. (2012). *Chronic absenteeism: Summarizing what we know from nationally available data.* Baltimore: Johns Hopkins University Center for Social Organization of Schools.

Balfanz, R., Fox, J. H., Bridgeland, J. M., & Bruce, M. (2013). *Grad nation community guidebook, Tool 9, Attendance survey.* Retrieved from http://guidebook.americaspromise.org/wp-content/uploads/2015/08/Tool-9-Attendance.pdf

Balfanz, R., Herzog, L., & Mac Iver, D. J. (2007). Preventing student disengagement and keeping students on the graduation path in urban middle-grades schools: Early identification and effective interventions. *Educational Psychologist, 42*(4), 223–235.

Barge, J. (2011). *Student attendance and student achievement.* Atlanta, GA: Georgia Department of Education.

Blazer, C. (2011). *Chronic absenteeism in the elementary grades* [Information Capsule 1009]. Miami, FL: Miami-Dade County Public Schools Research Services.

Brophy, J. (1986). Teacher influences on student achievement. *American Psychologist, 41*(10), 1069–1077.

Buehler, M. H., Tapogna, J., & Chang, H. N. (2012). *Why being in school matters: Chronic absenteeism in Oregon public schools.* Retrieved from http://www.attendanceworks.org/wordpress/wp-content/uploads/2012/02/Oregon-Research-Brief.pdf

Chang, H. N., & Jordan, P. W. (2011). Tackling chronic absence starting in the early grades: What cities can do to ensure that every child has a fighting chance to succeed. *National Civic Review, 100*(4), 6–12.

Chang, H. N., & Romero, M. (2008). *Present, engaged, and accounted for: The critical importance of addressing chronic absence in the early grades.* Retrieved from http://www.nccp.org/publications/pdf/text_837.pdf

Connolly, F., & Olson, L. S. (2012). *Early elementary performance and attendance in Baltimore City Schools' pre-kindergarten and kindergarten.* Baltimore: Baltimore Education Research Consortium.

Dalun, Z., Willson, V., Katsiyannis, A., Barrett, D., Song, J., & Jiun-Yu, W. (2010). Truancy offenders in the juvenile justice system: A multicohort study. *Behavioral Disorders, 35*(3), 229–242.

Dryfoos, J. G. (1990). *Adolescents at risk: Prevalence and prevention.* New York: Oxford University Press.

Easton, J. Q., & Engelhard, G., Jr. (1982). A longitudinal record of elementary school absence and its relationship to reading achievement. *Journal of Educational Research, 75*(5), 269–274.

Ehrlich, S. B., Gwynne, J. S., Pareja, A. S., & Allensworth, E. M. (2013). *Preschool attendance in Chicago Public Schools: Relationships with learning outcomes and reasons for absences.* Chicago: University of Chicago Consortium on Chicago School Research.

Farrington, D. P. (1996). Later life outcomes of truants in the Cambridge Study. In I. Berg & J. Nursten (Eds.), *Unwillingly to School* (4th ed., pp. 96–118). London: Gaskell/Royal College of Psychiatrists.

Garry, E. M. (1996). *Truancy: First step to a lifetime of problems.* Washington, DC: Office of Juvenile Justice and Delinquency Prevention, U.S. Department of Justice.

Get Schooled Foundation (2012). *Skipping to nowhere.* Retrieved from http://www.americaspromise.org/sites/default/files/d8/legacy/bodyfiles/Get%20Schooled%20Truancy%20Report.pdf

Ginsberg, A., Chang, H., & Jordan, P. (2014). *Absences add up: How school attendance influences student success.* Retrieved from http://www.attendanceworks.org/absences-add-up/

Gottfried, M. A., (2010). Evaluating the relationship between student attendance and achievement in urban elementary and middle schools: An instrumental variables approach. *American Educational Research Journal, 47*(2), 434–465.

Gottfried M. A. (2014). Chronic absenteeism and its effects on students' academic and socioemotional outcomes. *Journal of Education for Students Placed at Risk, 19*(2), 53–75.

Hallfors, D., Vevea, J. L., Iritani, B., Cho, H., Khatapoush, S., & Saxe, L. (2002). Truancy, grade point average, and sexual activity: A meta-analysis of risk indicators for youth substance use. *Journal of Social Health 72*(5), 205–211.

Hammond, C., Linton, D., Smink, J., & Drew, S. (2007). *Dropout risk factors and exemplary programs.* Clemson, SC: National Dropout Prevention Center, Communities in Schools.

Harvard Health Publishing. (2015, January). *Relaxation techniques: Breath control helps quell errant stress response.* Retrieved from https://www.health.harvard.edu/mind-and-mood/relaxation-techniques-breath-control-helps-quell-errant-stress-response

Hattie, J., & Timperley, H. (2007). The power of feedback. *Review of Educational Research, 77*(1), 81–112.

Henry, K. L., & Huizinga, D. H. (2007). Truancy's effect on the onset of drug use among urban adolescents placed at risk. *Journal of Adolescent Health, 40*(4), 358.e9–358.e17. doi: 10.1016/j.jadohealth.2006.11.138

Hibbett, A., Fogelman, K., & Manor, O. (1990). Occupational outcomes of truancy. *British Journal of Educational Psychology, 60*(1), 23–36.

Kane, J. (2006). School exclusions and masculine, working-class identities. *Gender and Education, 18*(6), 673–685.

Levin, H. M., & Belfield, C. R. (2007). Educational interventions to raise high school graduation rates. In H. M. Levin & C. R. Belfield (Eds.), *The price we pay: Economic and social consequences of inadequate education* (pp. 177–199). Washington, DC: Brookings Institution Press.

Loeber, R., & Farrington, D. (2000). Young children who commit crime: Epidemiology, developmental origins, risk factors, early interventions, and policy implications. *Development and Psychopathology, 12*(4), 737–762.

Maynard, B. R., Salas-Wright, C. P., & Vaughn, M. G. (2015). High school dropouts in emerging adulthood: Substance use, mental health problems, and crime. *Community Mental Health Journal, 51*(3), 289–299.

Musser, M. P. (2011). *Taking attendance seriously: How school absences undermine student and school performance in New York City.* Retrieved from http://graphics8.nytimes.com/packages/pdf/nyregion/20110617attendancereport.pdf

Nauer, K., White, A., & Yerneni, R. (2008). *Strengthening schools by strengthening families: Community strategies to reverse chronic absenteeism in the early grades and improve supports for children and families.* New York: Center for New York City Affairs, The New School.

Neild, R. C., Balfanz, R., & Herzog, L. (2007). An early warning system. *Educational Leadership, 65*(2), 28–33.

Reid, K. C. (1981). Alienation and persistent school absenteeism. *Research in Education, 26*(1), 31–40.

Robins, L. N., & Ratcliff, K. S. (1980). The long-term outcome of truancy. In L. A. Hersov & I. Berg (Eds.), *Out of school: Modern perspectives in truancy and school refusal* (pp. 65–83). New York: John Wiley.

Rocque, M., Jennings, W. G., Piquero, A. R., Ozkan, T., & Farrington, D. P. (2017). The importance of school attendance: Findings from the Cambridge Study in Delinquent Development on the Life-Course Effects of Truancy. *Crime & Delinquency, 63*(5), 592–612. doi: 10.1177/0011128716660520

Romero, M., & Lee, Y.-S. (2007). *A national portrait of chronic absenteeism in the early grades.* New York: National Center for Children in Poverty.

Rouse, C. E. (2007). Quantifying the costs of inadequate education: Consequences for the labor market. In C. R. Belfield & H. M. Levin (Eds.), *The price we pay: Economic and social consequences of inadequate education* (pp. 99–124). Washington, DC: Brookings Institution Press.

Rumberger, R., & Thomas, S. (2000). The distribution of dropout and turnover rates among urban and suburban high schools. *Sociology of Education, 73*(1), 39–67.

Shores, R. E., Gunter, P. L., & Jack, S. L. (1993). Classroom management strategies: Are they setting events for coercion? *Behavioral Disorders, 18*(2), 92–102.

Sparks, S. D. (2010). Districts begin looking harder at absenteeism. *Education Week*, 30(6), 1, 12–13.

Sprick, R. (2009). *CHAMPS: A proactive and positive approach to classroom management*. Eugene, OR: Ancora Publishing.

Sprick, R., & Garrison, M. (2008). *Interventions: Evidence-based behavioral strategies for individual students* (2nd ed.). Eugene, OR: Ancora Publishing.

Sprick, R., Isaacs, S., Booher, M., Sprick, J., & Rich, P. (2014). *Foundations: A proactive and positive behavior support system* (3rd ed., Modules A–F). Eugene, OR: Ancora Publishing.

Sprick, R., Knight, J., Reinke, W. M., Skyles, T., & Barnes, L. (2010). *Coaching classroom management* (2nd ed.). Eugene, OR: Ancora Publishing.

Sutherland, K. S., Lewis-Palmer, T., Stichter, J. P., & Morgan, P. L. (2008). Examining the influence of teacher behavior and classroom context on the behavioral and academic outcomes for students with emotional or behavioral disorders. *Journal of Special Education, 41*(4), 223–233.

U.S. Department of Education Office for Civil Rights. (2016). *Civil rights data collection (CRDC) for the 2013–14 school year.* Retrieved from https://www2.ed.gov/about/offices/list/ocr/docs/crdc-2013-14.html

Utah Education Policy Center, University of Utah. (2012). *Research brief: Chronic absenteeism.* Retrieved from https://www.schools.utah.gov/file/31291767-087c-4edb-8042-87f272507c1d

Index

The letter *f* following a page number denotes a figure.

absenteeism. *See* chronic absence
academic performance
lack of value of, 112
outcomes of chronic absence on, 12–14, 71*f*–73*f*
ADA (average daily attendance), 21–22
Alabiso, Jake, 19–20
alienation, 14–15
analyzing metrics, 35–38
Ancora Publishing, 7
anecdotal notes, 36–38
anonymous student surveys, 36, 37*f*
anxiety, 95, 110, 129–131
assigned seats, 26
at-risk attendance, 23
attendance charts, 43, 45*f*
attendance lessons
formal, 65
ideas for, 67–68, 69*f*–76*f*
planning, 66–67, 78–85
for specific skills, 68
timing of, 65–66
attendance squares system, 59–60
Attendopoly, 61–62
average daily attendance (ADA), 21–22
avoidance, 111
awards, 60

back-to-school night, 88
Barnes Elementary, 19–20
barriers to attendance, 110
Berenstain Bears' Trouble at School (Berenstain and Berenstain), 69*f*–70*f*
Berg, Tricia, 14–15

call logs, 97–98
campaigns
  classroom motivational systems, 42, 47–49
  defined, 40
  informal procedures for, 45–47
  launching, 41–45
  principles for, 49–54
  whole-class reinforcement systems, 55–62, 119–120
CHAMPS: A Proactive and Positive Approach to Classroom Management, 27–30
check-in/check-out (CICO), 114
chronic absence. *See also* truancy
  academic outcomes, 12–14
  brainstorming the negative impacts of, 11–12
  causes of, 110–112
  current findings on, 10–11
  defined, 22–23
  extracurricular outcomes, 15–16
  families and, 17
  intervention plans for, 101–114
  local communities and, 17–18
  metrics, 5
  other students and, 16–17
  reasons for, 3
  social-emotional outcomes, 14–15
  statistics on, 10–11
  support for, 114–115
  teachers and, 16
classrooms
  attendance records, 30–35
  climate of, 16–17
  discussions with, 38
classrooms (*continued*)
  motivational systems, 42, 47–49
  reinforcement systems, 55–62, 119–120
  routines for, 27
  trusting communities in, 16–17
color-coded phone call logs, 97–98
Common Core State Standards, 82*f*–85*f*
commonly used metrics, 20–22
communication, about attendance goals and data, 87–88, 97–98, 102, 103*f*
communities, effects of chronic absence on, 17–18
competitions, 60–61
conferences, 3, 92–93
Connections, 114
consecutive goals, 50–51
contingency plans, 53–54
corrective phone calls, 97–98
court proceedings, 3–4

daily classroom attendance graph, 55–56
daily progress report interventions, 114
data. *See also* metrics
  collecting, 20, 25–30, 36
  essential metrics, 5
  importance of, 19–20
  using, 66–67
"Dealing with Technology: Tips and Strategies for Families" handout, 94, 122–125
delinquent behavior, 15–16
depression, 110, 113–114
disabled students, 11

discussions
  class, 38
  individual, 102–107
dropouts, 18

early release/late start days, 74*f*–76*f*, 77
early-stage intervention plans, 101–109. *See also* intervention plans
education, lack of value of, 112
elementary students, attendance lesson ideas for, 69*f*–73*f*
employment, 15–16
end-of-day absences, 6–7
engagement strategies, 79–80
escape, 111
essential metrics, 5. *See also* data
evening and morning routines, 95
exclusion, 14–15
excused vs. unexcused absences, 21. *See also* truancy
extracurricular activities, 111–112
extracurricular outcomes of chronic absence, 15–16

families
  building relationships with, 96–99
  communication with, 87–96, 97–98, 102, 103*f*
  effects of chronic absence on, 17
  handouts for, 121–133
  meetings with, 3, 92–93
  permission of, 21
  vacations, 13
financial concerns, 110, 113
foster children, 11
function-based intervention plans, 109–110, 112–114. *See also* intervention plans

Garrison, Mickey, 102
goal setting, 49
grades. *See* academic performance
Graves, Heather, 61–62
greeting students, 45–46, 99

handouts
  "Dealing with Technology: Tips and Strategies for Families," 94, 122–125
  "Help Your Student Cope with Anxious Thoughts and Feelings: Relaxation and Anxiety Management Strategies," 95, 129–131
  "How Sick Is Too Sick for School?" 94, 126–127
  "Take the Stress Out of Your Morning Routine: Tips for Establishing Effective Bedtime and Morning Habits," 95, 132–133
  "Tips for Improving Your Child's Sleep and Reducing Absenteeism," 94–95, 128
"Help Your Student Cope with Anxious Thoughts and Feelings: Relaxation and Anxiety Management Strategies" handout, 95, 129–131
high school students, attendance lesson ideas for, 74*f*–76*f*
homeless students, 11, 113

"How Sick Is Too Sick for School?" handout, 94, 126–127

illness, 94, 110, 112–113, 126–127
individualized interventions, 102–107, 114
individualized metrics, 22–24
informal procedures, 45–47
initial attendance letters, 43, 44*f*
intervention plans
- early-stage, 101–109
- function-based, 109–110, 112–114
- support for, 114–115

Interventions (Sprick and Garrison), 102
invisible ink attendance rewards, 58–59

job performance, 15–16
juvenile court, 3–4

K–12 applications, 6, 69*f*–76*f*
kindergarten students
- academic outcomes of chronic absence on, 12–13
- attendance lesson ideas for, 69*f*–70*f*

late start days, 74*f*–76*f*, 77
lessons about attendance
- formal, 65
- ideas for, 67–68, 69*f*–76*f*
- planning, 66–67, 78–85
- potential topics, 82*f*–85*f*
- for specific skills, 68
- timing of, 65–66

letters home
- for chronic absence, 91*f*
- indicating each student's attendance rate, 89, 90*f*–91*f*
- initial attendance letter, 44*f*

local communities and society, effects of chronic absence on, 17–18
low-income homes, 11

makeup work, 16
mathematics standards, 82*f*–83*f*
McLean Elementary School, 52
meetings, 3, 92–93
mental health issues, 110, 113–114
messaging, 81–82
metrics
- analyzing, 35–38
- average daily attendance (ADA), 21–22
- chronic absence, 5
- classroom records of attendance, 30–35
- commonly used, 20–22
- essential, 5
- importance of, 19–20
- individualized, 22–24
- monitoring over time, 30–35, 107, 108*f*
- percentages versus number of days, 24–25
- recording, 25–30
- regular attendance, 5
- at-risk attendance, 23
- severe chronic absence, 24
- truancy, 21
- using, 66–67

middle school students, attendance lesson ideas for, 74*f*–76*f*
minority groups, 11
monitoring metrics over time, 30–35, 107, 108*f*
morning routines, 95
Morris, Jessica, 61–62
motivational systems, 47–49, 107–109, 119–120
mystery prizes, 48, 52–53, 58

newsletters, 89
number of days vs. percentages, 24–25

opportunities to respond (OTRs), 79–80
other students, effects of chronic absence on, 16–17

parents and families
  building relationships with, 96–99
  communication with, 87–96, 97–98, 102, 103*f*
  effects of chronic absence on, 17
  handouts for, 121–133
  meetings with, 3, 92–93
  permission of, 21
  vacations, 13
peers, effects of chronic absence on, 16–17
percentages vs. number of days, 24–25
phone calls, 45–46, 97–98, 102, 103*f*
poverty, 11
punitive approaches, 3–4

raffle system, 59
reading standards, 84*f*–85*f*
recording metrics, 25–30
records of attendance, 30–35
reflection writing activities, 38
regular attendance
  defined, 23
  metrics, 5
reinforcement systems
  ideas for, 119–120
  principles for, 49–54
  whole-class, 55–62, 119–120
reminders, 27
repeated practice opportunities, 80
rewards, 48–53, 60
risk-taking behavior, 15–16
roll call, 26

Safe & Civil Schools model, 4, 19, 23
School Leader's Guide to Tackling Attendance Challenges, 6, 10, 114
school personnel roles, 5
seating charts, 26
severe chronic absence, 24
shortened-days, 74*f*–76*f*, 77
sickness, 94, 110, 126–127
sleep habits, 94–95, 128
slogans, 41
small-group interventions, 114
social-emotional outcomes of chronic absence, 14–15
social media, communication via, 89
society, effects of chronic absence on, 17–18
Sprick, Jessica, 13, 14–15
Sprick, Randy, 102
start-of-class routines, 27

START on Time! program, 7
statistics on chronic absence, 10–11
students
- anonymous surveys of, 36, 37*f*
- assessments of understanding, 80–81
- changing behavior of, 4
- disabled, 11
- discussions with, 102–107
- elementary, 69*f*–73*f*
- greeting, 45–46, 99
- high school, 74*f*–76*f*
- homeless, 11, 113
- kindergarten, 12–13, 69*f*–70*f*
- middle school, 74*f*–76*f*
- support for, 114
- weekly attendance logs, 57*f*

substitute teachers, 26
suspension, effects on families, 17

"Take the Stress Out of Your Morning Routine: Tips for Establishing Effective Bedtime and Morning Habits" handout, 95, 132–133
tardies
- addressing, 6–7
- CHAMPS recommendations for, 27–30

teachers
- effects of chronic absence on, 16
- log of weekly attendance, 57*f*
- role of, 5
- substitute teachers, 26

technology use tips, 94, 122–125
test scores. *See* academic performance
"Tips for Improving Your Child's Sleep and Reducing Absenteeism" handout, 94–95, 128
traditional approaches, 3–4
transportation problems, 110, 113
truancy
- defined, 21
- measures of, 3

trusting class communities, 16–17

unexcused vs. excused absences, 21. *See also* truancy
U.S. Office for Civil Rights, 10
Utah, 11

vacations, 13

warm-up tasks, 27
whole-class reinforcement systems, 55–62, 119–120

About the Authors

Jessica Sprick, MS, Special Education, is a consultant and presenter for Safe & Civil Schools and a writer for Ancora Publishing. Ms. Sprick has been a special education teacher for students with behavioral needs and dean of students at the middle school level. Her practical experience in schools drives her passion to help school and district staff develop and implement effective behavioral, academic, and attendance approaches. Ms. Sprick is the lead trainer for the Safe & Civil Schools model of absenteeism prevention and intervention, and she is a coauthor of the following attendance resources: *School Leader's Guide to Tackling Attendance Challenges, Functional Behavior Assessment of Absenteeism & Truancy* and *Absenteeism & Truancy: Interventions and Universal Procedures.* Ms. Sprick is also a coauthor of *Foundations: A Proactive and Positive Behavior Support System* (3rd edition), *Functional Behavior Assessment of Bullying,* and *Bullying: Universal Procedures and Interventions.*

Tricia Berg, PhD, is a national and international education consultant who has worked with schools, districts, and states to develop multi-tiered systems of support for students. She has provided professional development and coaching support to educational organizations in the areas of math, explicit instruction, positive behavioral interventions and supports (PBIS), inclusive strategies, data-driven decision making, and special education compliance. Prior to becoming an education consultant, she worked as a district-level PBIS coordinator, behavior specialist, special education teacher, general education teacher, and paraprofessional. She has worked on research projects in the areas of mathematics, implementation and sustainability of PBIS, and attendance interventions. She received her PhD from the University of Oregon in special education with an emphasis on the relation between behaviors and academics, effective professional development practices, and effective interventions for students.

Related ASCD Resources

At the time of publication, the following resources were available (ASCD stock numbers appear in parentheses):

Print Products

School Leader's Guide to Tackling Attendance Challenges by Jessica Sprick and Randy Sprick (#118037)

Discipline with Dignity: How to Build Responsibility, Relationships, and Respect in Your Classroom, 4th edition by Richard L. Curwin, Allen N. Mendler, and Brian D. Mendler (#118018)

The Educator's Guide to Assessing and Improving School Discipline Programs by Mark Boynton and Christine Boynton (#107037)

Beyond Discipline: From Compliance to Community, 10th Anniversary Edition by Alfie Kohn (#106033)

Enhancing RTI: How to Ensure Success with Effective Classroom Instruction and Intervention by Douglas Fisher and Nancy Frey (#110037)

School Culture Rewired: How to Define, Assess, and Transform It by Steve Gruenert and Todd Whitaker (#115004)

How to Create a Culture of Achievement in Your School and Classroom by Douglas Fisher, Nancy Frey, & Ian Pumpian (#111014)

Building Your School's Capacity to Implement RTI: An ASCD Action Tool by Patricia Addison & Cynthia L. Warger (#111007)

Teaching with Poverty in Mind: What Being Poor Does to Kids' Brains and What Schools Can Do About It by Eric Jensen (#109074)

Hanging In: Strategies for Teaching the Students Who Challenge Us Most by Jeffrey Benson (#114013)

What Every School Leader Needs to Know About RTI by Margaret Searle (#109097)

Causes & Cures in the Classroom: Getting to the Root of Academic and Behavior Problems by Margaret Searle (#113019)

Everyday Engagement: Making Students and Parents Your Partners in Learning by Katy Ridnouer (#109009)

Turning High-Poverty Schools into High-Performing Schools by William Parrett and Kathleen Budge (#109003)

Better Than Carrots or Sticks: Restorative Practices for Positive Classroom Management by Dominique Smith, Douglas Fisher & Nancy Frey (#116005)

Fostering Resilient Learners: Strategies for Creating a Trauma-Sensitive Classroom by Kristin Souers with Pete Hall (#116014)

How to Reach the Hard to Teach: Excellent Instruction for Those Who Need It Most by Jana Echevarría, Nancy E. Frey, and Douglas B. Fisher (#116010)

Partnering with Parents to Ask the Right Questions: A Powerful Strategy for Strengthening School-Family Partnerships by Luz Santana, Dan Rothstein, and Agnes Bain (#117011)

For up-to-date information about ASCD resources, go to www.ascd.org. You can search the complete archives of *Educational Leadership* at www.ascd.org/el.

ASCD myTeachSource®
Download resources from a professional learning platform with hundreds of research-based best practices and tools for your classroom at http://myteachsource.ascd.org/.

For more information, send an e-mail to member@ascd.org; call 1-800-933-2723 or 703-578-9600; send a fax to 703-575-5400; or write to Information Services, ASCD, 1703 N. Beauregard St., Alexandria, VA 22311-1714 USA.